Cambridge
BEC Vantage
4

Park Campus
Library

WITH ANSWERS

Examination papers from
University of Cambridge
ESOL Examinations:
English for Speakers of
Other Languages

CAMBRIDGE
UNIVERSITY PRESS

REGENTS COLLEGE LIBRARY

17018773

CAMBRIDGE UNIVERSITY PRESS
Cambridge, New York, Melbourne, Madrid, Cape Town,
Singapore, São Paulo, Delhi, Mexico City

Cambridge University Press
The Edinburgh Building, Cambridge CB2 8RU, UK

www.cambridge.org
Information on this title: www.cambridge.org/9780521739269

© Cambridge University Press 2009

This publication is in copyright. Subject to statutory exception
and to the provisions of relevant collective licensing agreements,
no reproduction of any part may take place without the written
permission of Cambridge University Press.

First published 2009
3rd printing 2012

Printed in the United Kingdom at the University Press, Cambridge

A catalogue record for this book is available from the British Library

ISBN 978-0-521-73926-9 Student's Book with answers
ISBN 978-0-521-73927-6 Audio CD set
ISBN 978-0-521-73928-3 Self-study Pack

Cambridge University Press has no responsibility for the persistence or
accuracy of URLs for external or third-party internet websites referred to in
this publication, and does not guarantee that any content on such websites is,
or will remain, accurate or appropriate. Information regarding prices, travel
timetables and other factual information given in this work is correct at
the time of first printing but Cambridge University Press does not guarantee
the accuracy of such information thereafter.

REGENT'S COLLEGE
ACC No. 1 2 0 1 8 7 7 3
CLASS 428·24 VNI
S.I.
KEY ENGLISH LANGUAGE
EXAMINATIONS, QUESTIONS

Contents

Introduction

TO THE STUDENT

This book is for candidates preparing for the Cambridge Business English Certificate Vantage examination. It contains four complete tests based on past papers.

The BEC Suite

The Business English Certificates (BEC) are certificated examinations which can be taken on various dates throughout the year at approved Cambridge BEC centres. They are aimed primarily at individual learners who wish to obtain a business-related English language qualification, and provide an ideal focus for courses in Business English. Set in a business context, BEC tests English language, not business knowledge. BEC is available at three levels – Preliminary, Vantage and Higher.

The BEC Suite is linked to the five ALTE/Cambridge levels for language assessment, and to the Council of Europe's Framework for Modern Languages. It is also aligned with the UK Qualifications and Curriculum Authority's National Standards for Literacy, within the National Qualifications Framework (NQF).

BEC	Equivalent Main Suite Exam	Council of Europe Framework Level	UK NQF Level
	Certificate of Proficiency in English (CPE)	C2 (ALTE Level 5)	
BEC Higher	Certificate in Advanced English (CAE)	C1 (ALTE Level 4)	Level 2*
BEC Vantage	First Certificate in English (FCE)	B2 (ALTE Level 3)	Level 1
BEC Preliminary	Preliminary English Test (PET)	B1 (ALTE Level 2)	Entry 3
	Key English Test (KET)	A2 (ALTE Level 1)	

* This represents the level typically required for employment purposes to signify the successful completion of compulsory secondary education in the UK.

BEC Vantage

The BEC Vantage examination consists of four papers:

Reading	1 hour
Writing	45 minutes
Listening	40 minutes (approximately)
Speaking	14 minutes

Test of Reading (1 hour)

This paper consists of five parts with 45 questions, which take the form of two multiple-matching tasks, two multiple-choice tasks, and an error identification task. Part 1 contains four short texts or a longer text divided into four sections, and Parts 2, 3, 4 and 5 each contain one longer text. The texts are taken from newspapers, business magazines, business correspondence, books, leaflets, brochures, etc. They are all business-related, and are selected to test a wide range of reading skills and strategies.

Test of Writing (45 minutes)

For this paper, candidates are required to produce two pieces of writing. For Part 1, they write a note, message, memo or email to a colleague or colleagues within the company. For Part 2, they write a piece of business correspondence to somebody outside the company, a short report or a proposal. Candidates are asked to write 40 to 50 words for Part 1 and 120 to 140 words for Part 2.

Assessment is based on achievement of task, range and accuracy of vocabulary and grammatical structures, organisation, content, and appropriacy of register and format.

Test of Listening (approximately 40 minutes)

This paper consists of three parts with 30 questions, which take the form of a note-completion task, a multiple-matching task and a multiple-choice task. Part 1 contains three short conversations, Part 2 contains ten very short extracts, and Part 3 contains one longer text. The texts are audio recordings based on a variety of sources including interviews, telephone calls, face-to-face conversations and documentary features. They are all business-related, and are selected to test a wide range of listening skills and strategies.

Test of Speaking (14 minutes)

The Speaking test consists of three parts, which take the form of an interview section, a short presentation on a business topic, and a discussion. In the standard test format, candidates are examined in pairs by two examiners: an interlocutor and an assessor. The assessor awards a mark based on the following four criteria: Grammar and Vocabulary, Discourse Management, Pronunciation and Interactive Communication. The interlocutor provides a global mark for the whole test.

Marks and results

The four BEC Vantage papers total 120 marks, after weighting. Each paper is weighted to 30 marks. A candidate's overall grade is based on the total score gained in all four papers. It is not necessary to achieve a satisfactory level in all four papers in order to pass the examination. Certificates are given to candidates who pass the examination with grade A, B or C. A is the highest. The minimum successful performance in order to achieve a grade C corresponds to about 60% of the total marks. You will also be informed if you do particularly well in any individual paper. D and E are failing grades. Every candidate is provided with a

Statement of Results, which includes a graphical display of their performance in each paper. These are shown against the scale Exceptional – Good – Borderline – Weak and indicate the candidate's relative performance in each paper.

TO THE TEACHER

Candidature

Each year BEC is taken by over 120,000 candidates throughout the world. Most candidates are either already in work or studying in preparation for the world of work.

Content, preparation and assessment

Material used throughout BEC is as far as possible authentic and free of bias, and reflects the international flavour of the examination. The subject matter should not advantage or disadvantage certain groups of candidates, nor should it offend in areas such as religion, politics or sex.

TEST OF READING

Part	Main Skill Focus	Input	Response	No. of Questions
1	Reading – scanning and gist	One longer or four shorter informational texts (approx. 250–350 words in total)	Matching	7
2	Reading – understanding text structure	Single text: article, report, etc. with sentence-length gaps (text plus seven option sentences approx. 450–550 words in total)	Matching	5
3	Reading for gist and specific information	Single text (approx. 450–550 words)	4-option multiple choice	6
4	Reading – vocabulary and structure information	Single informational text with lexical gaps (text including gapped words approx. 200–300 words)	4-option multiple-choice cloze	15
5	Reading – understanding sentence structure / error identification	Short text (150–200 words) Identification of additional unnecessary words in text	Proof-reading	12

Reading Part One

This is a matching task. There are four short texts on a related theme (for example, descriptions of a group of products, or advertisements for jobs) or a single text divided into four sections. Although the context of each text will be similar, there will also be information that is particular to each text. The texts are labelled A–D. Candidates are presented with a set of seven items which are statements related to the texts. They are expected to match each statement with the relevant text. Questions in this part tend to focus mostly on the identification of specific information and detail. However, an item could focus on gist by testing areas such as the target reader or the topic.

Preparation
In order to prepare for this part, it would be useful to familiarise students with sets of short texts that have a similar theme. Newspapers, magazines and catalogues are useful sources in which to find such texts. Students should be encouraged to look closely at all the information, particularly as short texts often include additional snippets of information on separate lines (such as prices, dates, titles, measurements, etc.) that can easily be overlooked.

Students could be set questions which test global reading skills prior to reading the texts, so that they are trained to think automatically for whom a text is written and why it has been written.

Reading Part Two

This is a matching task, comprising a text that has had six sentences removed from it and a set of seven sentences labelled A–G. Candidates are required to match each gap with the sentence which they think fits in terms of meaning and structure. The first gap is always given as an example so that candidates have five gaps left to complete. When they have finished this part, there will be one sentence left which they have not used.

The texts for this part will have been chosen because they have a clear line of thought or argument that can still be discerned by the reader even with the sentences removed. When doing the task, therefore, students should be trained to read through the gapped text and the list of sentences first, in order to get an idea of what it is about. Having done that, they should be reassured that there is only one sentence that fits each gap.

This part is a test of text structure as well as meaning, and the gaps will be reasonably far apart, so that candidates can successfully anticipate the appropriate lexical and grammatical features of the missing sentence. Candidates can be expected to be tested on a variety of cohesive features with both a backward and forward reference, sometimes going beyond the sentence level. Thus, while selecting the appropriate sentence for a gap, they should read before and after the text to ensure that it fits well. At the end of this part, they should read through the entire text, inserting the gapped sentences as they go along, to ensure that the information is coherent.

Preparation
This can be quite a difficult task, especially for candidates who are unfamiliar with such an exercise. In preparing them for this part, it would be a good idea to select a number of graded texts that have clear, familiar ideas and evident cohesive features. Texts can be cut up, as they are in the test, or simply discussed in their entirety. In this way, students can work up to dealing with more complex material and identifying the many different ways that ideas are connected. It would also be useful when doing gapped texts to look at sentences that do not fit the gaps and discuss the reasons for this. Sometimes it

is possible to make a sentence fit a gap by simply changing a few words. Discussion on areas such as this would also be fruitful.

Reading Part Three

This task consists of a text accompanied by four-option multiple-choice items. The stem of a multiple-choice item may take the form of a question or an incomplete sentence. There are six items, which are placed after the text. The text is 450 to 550 words long. Sources of original texts may be the general and business press, company literature, and books on topics such as management. Texts may be edited, but the source is authentic.

Preparation
- Multiple-choice questions are a familiar and long-standing type of test; here, they are used to test opinion and inference rather than straightforward facts.
- Correct answers are not designed to depend on simple word-matching, and students' ability to interpret paraphrasing should be developed.
- Students should be encouraged to pursue their own interpretation of relevant parts of the text and then check their idea against the options offered, rather than reading all the options first.
- It could be useful for students to be given perhaps one of the wrong options only, and for them to try to write the correct answer and another wrong option.

Reading Part Four

This is a multiple-choice cloze test with 15 gaps, most of which test lexical items, and may focus on correct word choice, lexical collocations and fixed phrases. The texts chosen for this part will come from varied sources, but they will all have a straightforward message or meaning, so that candidates are being tested on vocabulary and not on their comprehension of the passage.

Preparation
Candidates are usually familiar with this type of task, and so it is most important to try and improve their range of vocabulary. The options provided in each item in the test will have similar meanings, but only one word will be correct within the context provided. Familiarity with typical collocations would be especially useful. The language of business is often very precise, and so it is worth spending time looking at the vocabulary used in different types of text, getting students to keep a vocabulary list and encouraging them to make active use of the lexical items that are new to them.

Reading Part Five

This is an error-correction or proof-reading task based on a text of 150 to 200 words, with 12 items. Candidates identify additional or unnecessary words in a text. This task can be related to the authentic task of checking a text for errors, and suitable text types are therefore letters, publicity materials, etc. The text is presented with 12 numbered lines, which are the lines containing the items. Further lines at the end may complete the text, but they are not numbered.

Preparation

- Students should be reminded that this task represents a kind of editing that is common practice, even in their first language.
- Any work on error analysis is likely to be helpful for this task.
- It may well be that photocopies of students' own writing could provide an authentic source for practice.
- A reverse of the exercise (giving students texts with missing words) might also prove beneficial.

Marks

One mark is given for each correct answer. The total score is then weighted to 30 marks for the whole Reading paper.

TEST OF WRITING

Part	Functions/Communicative Task	Input	Response	Register
1	e.g. giving instructions, explaining a development, asking for comments, requesting information, agreeing to requests	Rubric only (plus layout of output text type)	Internal communication (medium may be note, message, memo or email) (40–50 words)	Neutral/ informal
2	Report: describing, summarising Correspondence: e.g. explaining, apologising, reassuring, complaining Proposal: describing, summarising, recommending, persuading	One or more pieces of input from: business correspondence (medium may be letter, fax or email), internal communication (medium may be note, memo or email), notice, advert, graphs, charts, etc. (plus layout if output is fax or email)	Business correspondence (medium may be letter, fax or email) or short report or proposal (medium may be memo or email) (120–140 words)	Neutral/ formal

For BEC Vantage, candidates are required to produce two pieces of writing:
- an internal company communication; this means a piece of communication with a colleague or colleagues within the company on a business-related matter, and the delivery medium may be a note, message, memo or email;
- one of the following:
  - a report; this means the presentation of information in relation to a specific issue or event. The report will contain an introduction, main body of findings and conclusion; it is possible that the delivery medium may be a memo or an email;
  - a piece of business correspondence; this means correspondence with somebody outside the company (e.g. a customer or supplier) on a business-related matter, and the delivery medium may be a letter, fax or email;
  - a proposal; this has a similar format to a report, but unlike the report, the focus of the proposal is on the future, with the main focus being on recommendations for discussion; it is possible that the delivery medium may be a memo or an email.

Writing Part One

In the first task, candidates are presented with the context in the task rubric. This explains the role the candidate must take in order to write a note, message, memo or email of around 40 to 50 words using a written prompt. It also identifies who the message is to be written to. The prompt will be included in the instructions in the rubric and will be in the form of bullet points clearly stating the pieces of information that must be incorporated into the answer.

Writing Part Two

In the second Writing task, candidates are required to write 120 to 140 words, which will be in the form of business correspondence, a short report or proposal. There will be an explanation of the task and one or more texts as input material. These texts may contain visual or graphic material, and have 'handwritten' notes on them.

Preparing for the Writing paper

Students should have practice in the clear and concise presentation of written information. Exposure to, and discussion of, as wide a range as possible of relevant texts would be beneficial. Students should be trained to consider:
- the target reader
- references to previous communication
- the purpose of writing
- the requirements of the format (e.g. letter, report)
- the main points to be addressed
- the approximate number of words to be written for each point
- suitable openings and closings
- the level of formality required.

It is important that students are aware of the need to reformulate the wording of the content points/handwritten notes given in the task, in order to include original vocabulary and structures, since evidence of a range of structures and vocabulary is one of the marking criteria.

Assessment

An impression mark is awarded to each piece of writing. The General Impression Mark Scheme is used in conjunction with a task-specific mark scheme, which focuses on criteria specific to each particular task. This summarises the content, organisation, register, format and target reader indicated in the task.

The band scores awarded are translated to a mark out of 10 for Part 1 and a mark out of 20 for Part 2. A total of 30 marks is available for Writing.

The General Impression Mark Scheme is interpreted at Council of Europe Level B2.

A summary of the General Impression Mark Scheme is reproduced opposite. Examiners work with a more detailed version, which is subject to regular updating.

General Impression Mark Scheme – Writing

Band	
5	Full realisation of the task set. • All content points included and expanded upon where the task allows. • Controlled, natural use of language; minimal errors, which are minor. • Wide range of structures and vocabulary. • Effectively organised, with appropriate use of cohesive devices. • Register and format consistently appropriate. Very positive effect on the reader.
4	Good realisation of the task set. • All content points adequately dealt with. • Generally accurate; errors when complex language is attempted. • Good range of structures and vocabulary. • Generally well organised, with attention paid to cohesion. • Register and format on the whole appropriate. Positive effect on the reader.
3	Reasonable achievement of the task set. • All major content points included; some minor omissions. • A number of errors will be present, but they do not impede communication. • Adequate range of structures and vocabulary. • Organisation and cohesion are satisfactory, on the whole. • Register and format reasonable, although not entirely successful. Satisfactory effect on the reader.
2	Inadequate attempt at the task set. • Some major content points omitted or inadequately dealt with; some irrelevance is likely. • Errors sometimes obscure communication, are numerous, and distract the reader. • Limited range of structures and vocabulary. • Content is not clearly organised or linked, causing some confusion. • Inappropriate register and format. Negative effect on the reader.
1	Poor attempt at the task set. • Notable content omissions and/or considerable irrelevance, possibly due to misinterpretation of the task set. • Serious lack of control; frequent basic errors. • Little evidence of structures and vocabulary required by task. • Lack of organisation, causing a breakdown in communication. • Little attempt at appropriate register and format. Very negative effect on the reader.
0	Achieves nothing. Either fewer than 25% of the required number of words or totally illegible or totally irrelevant.

TEST OF LISTENING

Part	Main Skill Focus	Input	Response	No. of Questions
1	Listening for writing short answers	Three telephone conversations or messages	Gap-filling	12
2	Listening; identifying topic, context, function, etc.	Short monologue; two sections of five 'snippets' each	Multiple matching	10
3	Listening	One extended conversation or monologue; interview, discussion, presentation, etc.	Multiple choice	8

Listening Part One

In this part, there are three conversations or answering-machine messages, with a gapped text to go with each. Each gapped text provides a very clear context and has four spaces which have to be filled with one or two words, or a number. The gapped texts may include forms, diary excerpts, invoices, message pads, etc. Candidates hear each conversation or message twice and as they listen they are required to complete the gapped text.

This part of the Listening test concentrates on the retrieval of factual information and it is important for candidates to listen carefully using the prompts on their question paper in order to identify the missing information. For example, they may have to note down a person's name, and if names on the recording are spelt out, those answers must be spelt correctly. Alternatively, they may have to listen for a room or telephone number, or an instruction or deadline. Answers to this part are rarely a simple matter of dictation and some reformulation of the prompt material will be required in order to locate the correct answer.

Listening Part Two

This part is divided into two sections. Each section has the same format: candidates hear five short monologues and have to match each monologue to a set of items, A–H. In each section, the eight options will form a coherent set and the overall theme or topic will be clearly stated in the task rubric. For example, candidates may hear five people talking and have to decide what sort of jobs the people do. Hence, the set of options A–H will contain a list of jobs. Alternatively, the set of options may consist of eight places/topics/addressees/purposes, etc. The two sections will always test different areas and so, if the first section focuses on, say, topics, the second section will focus on something else, such as functions.

In this part of the Listening test, candidates are being tested on their global listening skills and also on their ability to infer, extract gist and understand main ideas. In order to answer the questions successfully, they will need to work out the answer by developing ideas, and refining these as the text is heard. It will not be possible to 'word-match' and candidates should not expect to hear such overt cues. However, there will always be a 'right' answer and candidates are not expected to opt for the 'best' answer.

Listening Part Three

A longer text is heard in this part, usually lasting approximately four minutes. The text will typically be an interview, conversation or discussion with two or more speakers, or possibly a presentation or report with one speaker. There are eight, three-option multiple-choice questions that focus on details and main ideas in the text. There may be questions on opinions and feelings but these will be relatively straightforward and will not require candidates to remember long or complex pieces of information.

Preparing for the Listening paper

All listening practice should be helpful for students, whether authentic or specially prepared. In particular, discussion should focus on:
- the purpose of speeches and conversations or discussions
- the speakers' roles
- the opinions expressed
- the language functions employed
- relevant aspects of phonology such as stress, linking and weak forms, etc.
  In addition, students should be encouraged to appreciate the differing demands of each task type. It will be helpful not only to practise the task types in order to develop a sense of familiarity and confidence, but also to discuss how the three task types relate to real-life skills and situations:
- the first is note-taking (and therefore productive), and students should reflect on the various situations in which they take notes from a spoken input. They should also be encouraged to try to predict the kinds of words or numbers that might go in the gaps;
- the second is a matching (with discrimination) exercise, and reflects the ability to interrelate information between reading and listening and across differing styles and registers;
- the third involves the correct interpretation of spoken input, with correct answers often being delivered across different speakers.
  In all three tasks, successful listening depends on correct reading, and students should be encouraged to make full use of the pauses during the test to check the written input.

Marks

One mark is given for each correct answer, giving a total score of 30 marks for the whole Listening paper.

TEST OF SPEAKING

Part	Format/Content	Time	Interaction Focus
1	Conversation between the interlocutor and each candidate Giving personal information; talking about present circumstances, past experiences and future plans, expressing opinions, speculating, etc.	About 3 minutes	The interlocutor encourages the candidates to give information about themselves and to express personal opinions.
2	A 'mini presentation' by each candidate on a business theme Organising a larger unit of discourse Giving information and expressing and justifying opinions	About 6 minutes	Each candidate is given prompts which they use to prepare and give a short talk on a business-related topic.
3	Two-way conversation between candidates followed by further prompting from the interlocutor Expressing and justifying opinions, speculating, comparing and contrasting, agreeing and disagreeing, etc.	About 5 minutes	The candidates are presented with a business-related situation to discuss. The interlocutor extends the discussion with prompts on related topics.

The Speaking test is conducted by two oral examiners (an interlocutor and an assessor), with pairs of candidates. The interlocutor is responsible for conducting the Speaking test and is also required to give a mark for each candidate's performance during the whole test. The assessor is responsible for providing an analytical assessment of each candidate's performance and, after being introduced by the interlocutor, takes no further part in the interaction.

The Speaking test is designed for pairs of candidates. However, where a centre has an uneven number of candidates, the last three candidates will be examined together.

Speaking Part One

In the first part of the test, the interlocutor addresses each candidate in turn and asks first general, then more business-related questions. Candidates will not be addressed in strict sequence. This part of the test takes about three minutes and during this time candidates are tested on their ability to talk briefly about themselves, and to perform functions such as agreeing and disagreeing, and expressing preferences.

Speaking Part Two

The second part of the test is a 'mini presentation'. In this part, the candidates are given a choice of topic and have a minute to prepare a presentation of approximately one minute. After each candidate has spoken, their partner is invited to ask a question about what has been said.

Speaking Part Three

The third part of the test is a discussion between candidates. The interlocutor gives candidates a business-related situation to discuss. The candidates are asked to speak for about three minutes. The interlocutor will support the conversation as appropriate and then ask further questions related to the main theme.

Preparing for the Speaking test

It is important to familiarise candidates with the format of the test before it takes place, by the use of paired and group activities in class. Teachers may need to explain the benefits of this type of assessment to candidates. The primary purpose of paired assessment is to sample a wider range of discourse than can be elicited from an individual interview.

In the first part of the test, candidates mainly respond to questions or comments from the interlocutor. Students need practice in exchanging personal and non-personal information; at Vantage level, it may be possible for students to practise talking about themselves in pairs or groups with or without prompts (such as written questions). However, prompt materials are necessary for Parts Two and Three, and students could be encouraged to design these themselves or may be provided with specially prepared sets. In small classes, students could discuss authentic materials as a group prior to engaging in pairwork or group activities. Such activities can familiarise students with the types of interactive skills involved in asking and providing factual information, such as: speaking clearly, formulating questions, listening carefully and giving precise answers.

In the 'mini presentation', candidates are asked to show an ability to talk for an extended period of time. Discussion activities, as well as giving short talks or presentations, can help to develop this skill.

In the final discussion in the Vantage Speaking test, candidates are also tested on their ability to express opinions, to compare and contrast, to concede points and possibly to reach a conclusion (although it is perfectly acceptable for candidates to agree to differ). Any discussion activities on a business theme that encourage students to employ these skills are likely to be beneficial. Group or class discussions can be valuable ways of developing these skills.

Assessment

Candidates are assessed on their own performance and not in relation to each other according to the following analytical criteria: Grammar and Vocabulary, Discourse Management, Pronunciation and Interactive Communication. These criteria are interpreted at Vantage level. Assessment is based on performance in the whole test and is not related to particular parts of the test.

Both examiners assess the candidates. The assessor applies detailed analytical scales, and the interlocutor applies a Global Achievement Scale, which is based on the analytical scales. The analytical criteria are further described below.

Grammar and Vocabulary

This refers to range and accuracy as well as the appropriate use of grammatical and lexical forms. At BEC Vantage level, a range of grammar and vocabulary is needed to deal with the tasks. At this level, candidates should be accurate enough, and use sufficiently appropriate vocabulary, to convey their intended meanings.

Discourse Management

This refers to the coherence, extent and relevance of each candidate's individual performance. Contributions should be adequate to deal with the BEC Vantage level tasks.

Pronunciation

This refers to the candidate's ability to produce comprehensible utterances. At BEC Vantage level, meanings are conveyed through the appropriate use of stress, rhythm, intonation and clear individual sounds.

Interactive Communication

This refers to the candidate's ability to take an active part in the development of the discourse. At BEC Vantage level, candidates should be sensitive to turn-taking and sustain the interaction by initiating and responding appropriately.

Global Achievement Scale

This refers to the candidate's overall performance throughout the test. Throughout the Speaking test, candidates are assessed on their language skills and, in order to be able to make a fair and accurate assessment of each candidate's performance, the examiners must be given an adequate sample of language to assess. Candidates must, therefore, be prepared to provide full answers to the questions asked by either the interlocutor or the other candidate, and to speak clearly and audibly. While it is the responsibility of the interlocutor, where necessary, to manage or direct the interaction, thus ensuring that both candidates are given an equal opportunity to speak, it is the responsibility of the candidates to maintain the interaction as much as possible. Candidates who take equal turns in the interchange will utilise to best effect the amount of time available.

Grading and results

Grading takes place once all scripts have been returned to Cambridge ESOL and marking is complete. This is approximately five weeks after the examination. There are two main stages: grading and awards.

Grading

The four papers total 120 marks, after weighting. Each skill represents 25% of the total marks available. The grade boundaries (A, B, C, D and E) are set using the following information:
- statistics on the candidature
- statistics on the overall candidate performance

- statistics on individual items, for those parts of the examination for which this is appropriate (Reading and Listening)
- the advice of the Principal Examiners, based on the performance of candidates, and on the recommendation of examiners where this is relevant (Writing)
- comparison with statistics from previous years' examination performance and candidature.

A candidate's overall grade is based on the total score gained in all four papers. It is not necessary to achieve a satisfactory level in all four papers in order to pass the examination.

Awards

The Awarding Committee deals with all cases presented for special consideration, e.g. temporary disability, unsatisfactory examination conditions, suspected collusion, etc. The Committee can decide to ask for scripts to be re-marked, to check results, to change grades, to withhold results, etc. Results may be withheld because of infringement of regulations or because further investigation is needed. Centres are notified if a candidate's results have been scrutinised by the Awarding Committee.

Results

Results are reported as three passing grades (A, B and C) and two failing grades (D and E). The minimum successful performance which a candidate typically requires in order to achieve a Grade C corresponds to about 60% of the total marks. Candidates are given a Statement of Results which, in addition to their grades, shows a graphical profile of their performance on each paper. These are shown against the scale Exceptional – Good – Borderline – Weak and indicate the candidate's relative performance in each paper. Certificates are issued to passing candidates after the issue of the Statement of Results and there is no limit on the validity of the certificates.

Further information

For more information about BEC or any other Cambridge ESOL examination, write to:

University of Cambridge ESOL Examinations
1 Hills Road
Cambridge
CB1 2EU
United Kingdom

Tel: +44 1223 553997
Fax: +44 1223 553621
email: ESOLHelpdesk@ucles.org.uk
website: www.CambridgeESOL.org

In some areas, this information can also be obtained from the British Council.

Test 1

READING   1 hour

PART ONE

Questions 1–7

- Look at the statements below and the article about the development of future business leaders on the opposite page.
- Which section of the article (**A, B, C** or **D**) does each statement (**1–7**) refer to?
- For each statement (**1–7**), mark one letter (**A, B, C** or **D**) on your Answer Sheet.
- You will need to use some of these letters more than once.

Example:

0   A new organisation has been formed to assist firms in developing high-flyers.

---

1   Managers need to take action to convince high-flyers of their value to the firm.

2   Organisations need to look beyond the high-flyers they are currently developing.

3   There is a concern that firms investing in training for high-flyers may not gain the benefits themselves.

4   Managers need expert assistance from within their own firms in developing high-flyers.

5   Firms currently identify high-flyers without the support of a guidance strategy.

6   Managers are frequently too busy to deal with the development of high-flyers.

7   Firms who work hard on their reputation as an employer will interest high-flyers.

The Stars of the Future

A   Existing management research does not tell us much about how to find and develop high-flyers, those people who have the potential to reach the top of an organisation. As a result, organisations are left to formulate their own systems. A more effective overall policy for developing future leaders is needed, which is why the London Business School has launched the Tomorrow's Leaders Research Group (TLRG). The group contains representatives from 20 firms, and meets regularly to discuss the leadership development of the organisations' high-flyers.

B   TLRG recognises just how significant line managers are in the process of leadership development. Unfortunately, with today's flat organisations, where managers have functional as well as managerial responsibilities, people development all too often falls victim to heavy workloads. One manager in the research group was unconvinced by the logic of sending his best people away on development courses, 'only to see them poached by another department or, worse still, another firm'. This fear of losing high-flyers runs deep in the organisations that make up the research group.

C   TLRG argues that the task of management is not necessarily about employee retention, but about creating 'attraction centres'. 'We must help line managers to realise that if their companies are known as ones that develop their people, they will have a greater appeal to high-flyers,' said one advisor. Furthermore, selecting people for, say, a leadership development programme is a sign of commitment from management to an individual. Loyalty can then be more easily demanded in return.

D   TLRG has concluded that a company's HR specialists need to take action and engage with line managers individually about their role in the development of high-flyers. Indeed, in order to benefit fully from training high-flyers as the senior managers of the future, firms must actually address the development of all managers who will be supporting the high-flyers. Without this, managers will not be in a position to give appropriate advice. And when eventually the high-flyers do move on, new ones will be needed to replace them. The next challenge will be to find a new generation of high-flyers.

PART TWO

Questions 8–12

- Read the article below about possible reasons for acquiring a company.
- Choose the best sentence from the opposite page to fill each of the gaps.
- For each gap (**8–12**), mark one letter (**A–G**) on your Answer Sheet.
- Do not use any letter more than once.
- There is an example at the beginning (**0**).

ACQUISITION
When should a company consider acquisition as a way forward?

There are many circumstances in which a company may wish to take over another organisation through an acquisition.

The need to keep up with a changing environment often dominates thinking about acquisitions. One compelling reason to develop by acquisition is the speed with which it allows the company to enter new product or market areas. (**0**) .....G..... This is particularly true of e-commerce.

The strength of competitors may influence a company to choose acquisition as a way forward. In markets that are static and where market shares of companies are reasonably steady, it can be difficult for a company to break into the market, since its presence may create excess capacity. (**8**) ....

The same arguments also apply˘ when an established supplier in an industry acquires a competitor. This may either be to gain the competitor's market share or, in some cases, to shut down its capacity in order to restore a situation where supply and demand are more balanced.

There may be financial motives for acquisition. If the share value of a company is high, the motive may be to spot and acquire a firm with a low share value. (**9**) .... An extreme example is asset stripping, where the main motive for the acquisition is short-term gain by buying up undervalued assets and selling them on bit by bit.

There may also be resource considerations. There may be a lack of resources or skills to compete successfully, so they must be acquired. (**10**) .... It may also be that it has knowledge of a particular type of production system, business process or market need. In an international context, acquisition is often a means of gaining market knowledge.

Sometimes there are reasons of cost efficiency which make acquisition look attractive. A cost efficiency could arise from the fact that an established company may already be very experienced and have achieved efficiencies which another company would find difficult to achieve quickly by internal means. (**11**) .... In consumer goods industries, cost efficiency is usually the reason for an acquisition.

Acquisition can also be driven by the expectations of key shareholders. Shareholders usually expect to see continuing growth, and acquisition may be a quick way to deliver this growth. But there are considerable dangers that an acquisition can lower share price rather than increase it. (**12**) .... This is more likely when the decision to acquire is speculative as opposed to strategic. There are some shareholders who favour acquisition simply to bring a short-term boost to share value.

Example:

0	A	B	C	D	E	F	G
	☐	☐	☐	☐	☐	☐	▬

A   The necessary development and organisational learning would be too slow.

B   In the same way, an organisation can increase manufacturing opportunities.

C   Indeed, this is one of the major reasons for the more speculative acquisitions that take place.

D   It may be that the parent company may not have sufficient understanding of the acquired business, and this could remove value.

E   For example, a company may be taken over for its research and development expertise.

F   If, however, the company enters by acquisition, the risk of reaction from industry rivals is reduced.

G   In some cases, a market is changing so fast that acquisition becomes the only way of successfully breaking into it.

PART THREE

Questions 13–18

- Read the article below about changing attitudes to creativity in the workplace, and the questions on the opposite page.
- For each question (**13–18**), mark one letter (**A**, **B**, **C** or **D**) on your Answer Sheet.

CREATIVITY IN THE WORKPLACE

Nowadays, many UK companies are striving to be more creative. But according to a recent survey of senior managers, the lack of a can-do mentality amongst employees and an aversion to risk is hindering British business. Many think there is too much focus on delivering results quickly, which leaves insufficient time to think creatively. Some complain that a lack of coherent vision on creativity prevents their organisation from being more innovative.

Yet while senior managers may regret the lack of creativity, they must take much of the blame for creating the situation. Until recently, successive generations of management ignored innovative ideas from employees. Indeed, new ways of thinking were often regarded as an unwanted distraction, and original thinkers received little support. Despite the fact that many organisations are now taking steps to re-orient the business culture to promote creativity, it is not surprising, given this background, that a creative environment is hard to establish.

Another related issue is raised by Katrina Murray, a partner in a management consultancy: 'While many senior managers still complain about the lack of support for creativity in their organisations, they also fail to appreciate the contribution that they themselves can make. In some companies, there is a perception that only managers at board level can influence the company culture.' Murray feels that such organisations are unlikely to change. For her, 'creative organisations are made up of individuals who believe they can dictate their own future. Companies need to be able to spot these individuals and gently encourage them to lead the way.'

It is also necessary for senior managers to re-examine their role. According to Alex Sadowski, an American professor of management science,

'promoting creativity means re-evaluating most of what we know about management. It means organisations must be prepared to invest in ideas without being sure of the return on that investment.' Katrina Murray agrees with this view. 'Businesses are expert at the measured approach, which involves analysis and risk avoidance. But there is another approach, which involves intuition and not always looking at the bottom line. What is hard is establishing a working environment in which both these approaches can function simultaneously.'

Nevertheless, there are some pleasing indicators of progress in this area. Many of the senior managers interviewed in the survey say their organisations have adopted a number of strategies to encourage individuals to channel their creativity. Among these are giving open and honest feedback, allowing employees the freedom to measure their performance against more flexible goals, and higher toleration levels of failure. Senior managers also recognise that the way an organisation is led and managed is critical to building a creative environment and that they themselves have an important role to play.

But there are some experts who believe an even more fundamental change is needed. Tom Robertson, a professor of creative education, believes that the lack of creativity in companies is a problem that originated in schools and universities. The solution, he says, lies in more enlightened educational policies. 'There are already signs of this, but creativity is still concentrated in certain sectors, such as pharmaceuticals, advertising and the media. These sectors have always valued creativity, but the real challenge will be to shift some of these sectors' practices into more traditional manufacturing and service companies.'

13   Many senior managers feel that organisations have difficulties innovating because of

    A   a poor level of skills among employees.

    B   an emphasis on rapid achievement.

    C   an increased risk associated with change.

    D   an insistence on a standard company philosophy.

14   According to the writer, many organisations today are

    A   finding it easier to introduce a creative approach.

    B   having problems understanding innovation as a concept.

    C   actively developing the conditions for a creative approach.

    D   resisting innovative staff suggestions.

15   In the third paragraph, Katrina Murray expresses the view that

    A   top management must dictate the pace of change.

    B   some employees lack a commitment to change.

    C   most organisations are incapable of bringing about effective change.

    D   some senior managers underestimate the role they can play in achieving change.

16   Alex Sadowski and Katrina Murray agree that to be truly innovative, organisations must

    A   invest in the right managers.

    B   place less emphasis on financial considerations.

    C   have a double focus to their policies.

    D   adopt an approach with clearly defined stages.

17   According to the survey, which of the following strategies has been introduced to encourage creativity?

    A   a greater acceptance of error

    B   financial rewards for higher levels of creativity

    C   the introduction of specific performance targets

    D   the promotion of creative individuals to senior posts

18   Tom Robertson believes that, in the future, it will be difficult to achieve

    A   an educational system that encourages creativity.

    B   a combination of practices that promote creativity.

    C   the spread of creativity to a range of businesses.

    D   a greater respect for creativity in pharmaceutical companies.

PART FOUR

Questions 19–33

- Read the article below about doing business online.
- Choose the best word or phrase to fill each gap from **A**, **B**, **C** or **D** on the opposite page.
- For each question (**19–33**), mark one letter (**A**, **B**, **C** or **D**) on your Answer Sheet.
- There is an example at the beginning (**0**).

The Secret of Success for Online Businesses

The secret of success in electronic commerce (**0**) .....B..... in placing a new emphasis on a well-established area. That area is customer service, which is now the only point of (**19**) .... between a business and the buying public.

There are a number of factors in a real-world shop that (**20**) .... people's perceptions of a business: these (**21**) .... the location and the appearance of the premises, the quality and the pricing of the merchandise or services, and the behaviour of the staff.

However, if a company is trying to make a good impression with online customers, most of these factors do not (**22**) .... a part. In the (**23**) .... of these factors, the way customers are (**24**) .... when they have a reason to call has a fundamental effect on a company's ability to retain them as customers. Even more than regular telephone or in-person customers, web customers are impatient, easily frustrated and always conscious that they have other places where they can (**25**) .... their business. Preventing them from doing that means meeting them on their own (**26**) .... and providing them with what they want.

This necessity, in (**27**) .... , means that companies that sell over the net must get back-end functions right. Imposing (**28**) .... requirements on customers will not work; a business that (**29**) .... on customers emailing for assistance instead of using the phone, for example, will lose repeat custom.

If the phone is used, it must be answered (**30**) .... , and the staff should look for ways of helping even the most awkward customers (**31**) .... , as is more usual, trying to find some (**32**) .... to blame the customer for any problem.

An important, final point is that it is vital that all addresses, web links and phone numbers work properly and efficiently. This ought to (**33**) .... without saying. Experience, however, shows that it does not.

Example:

A stays   B lies   C exists   D stems

0	A	B	C	D
	▭	▬	▭	▭

19 A relationship   B association   C meeting   D contact

20 A force   B determine   C decide   D fix

21 A enclose   B consist   C include   D contain

22 A get   B run   C play   D have

23 A absence   B lack   C need   D scarcity

24 A cared   B treated   C dealt   D considered

25 A deliver   B bring   C move   D take

26 A policies   B standards   C terms   D conditions

27 A turn   B sequence   C line   D order

28 A dense   B rigid   C deep   D solid

29 A demands   B insists   C expects   D instructs

30 A punctually   B precisely   C promptly   D presently

31 A apart from   B other than   C except for D rather than

32 A case   B excuse   C fault   D purpose

33 A do   B make   C go   D come

PART FIVE

Questions 34–45

- Read the advice below about meetings with clients.
- In most of the lines (**34–45**), there is one extra word. It either is grammatically incorrect or does not fit in with the meaning of the text. Some lines, however, are correct.
- If a line is correct, write **CORRECT** on your Answer Sheet.
- If there is an extra word in the line, write **the extra word** in CAPITAL LETTERS on your Answer Sheet.
- The exercise begins with two examples (**0** and **00**).

Examples:	**0**	C	O	R	R	E	C	T	
	00	W	I	T	H				

Client Meetings

0 Regular meetings with clients are important to a healthy collaboration. They

00 may be set up by the client, for example to review with the progress of current

34 projects, to give new instructions that may have lead to a contract variation

35 or to discuss any concerns. The client meeting which can also be arranged

36 by you or another member of your company to attract from new business, to

37 address a problem unless that needs to be solved or to give an update or status

38 report on current business ventures. Your part is in these meetings will dictate

39 the kind of information you need and how you should prepare for them. If you

40 will be responding to questions put by your client, the material you present

41 should deal in specifically with the request that was made. The meeting should not

42 only move off the agenda without the permission of the person you are meeting.

43 If you have prepared properly, you should be able to anticipate both questions and

44 to respond properly. If you are put on the spot and asked for details you do not

45 have, respond honestly – do not speak about matters as you are not familiar with.

WRITING   45 minutes

PART ONE

- You are organising a meeting to discuss possible cuts to your department's budget.
- Write an **email** to all staff in your department:
  - giving them the date of the meeting
  - explaining why some cuts have to be made
  - saying why it is important for all staff to attend.
- Write **40–50** words.

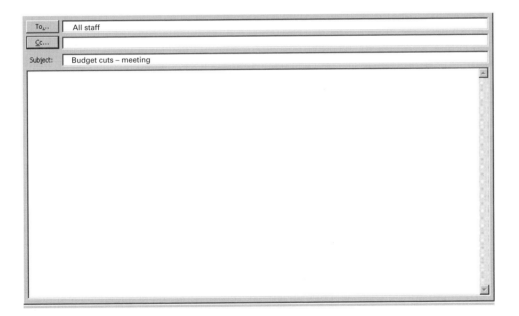

PART TWO

- The retail company you work for is considering installing a TV system in its store to give customers information on products and services while they shop. You have seen an advertisement for a company which provides this type of system.
- Look at the information below, on which you have already made some handwritten notes.
- Then, using **all** your handwritten notes, write a **letter** to Chris Taylor at TVInfoSystems.
- Write **120–140** words.

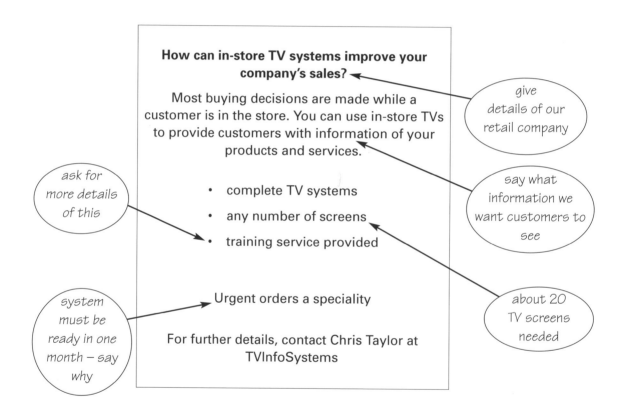

How can in-store TV systems improve your company's sales?

Most buying decisions are made while a customer is in the store. You can use in-store TVs to provide customers with information of your products and services.

- complete TV systems
- any number of screens
- training service provided

Urgent orders a speciality

For further details, contact Chris Taylor at TVInfoSystems

give details of our retail company

say what information we want customers to see

ask for more details of this

about 20 TV screens needed

system must be ready in one month – say why

LISTENING   40 minutes (including 10 minutes' transfer time)

PART ONE

Questions 1–12

- You will hear three telephone conversations or messages.
- Write **one** or **two** words or a number in the numbered spaces on the notes or forms below.
- After you have listened once, replay each recording.

Conversation One

(Questions 1–4)

- Look at the note below.
- You will hear a man phoning a customer about an order.

MESSAGE

To: Bob Cole

From: Alex Parker at Pilton Engineering

- The delivery date for our new **(1)** .... machines has been delayed.

- He asked if we needed to apply the **(2)** .... in the contract on this occasion.

- He is now offering free **(3)** ....

- One thing not clear in the contract – who is responsible for **(4)** .... during transit?

Conversation Two

(Questions 5–8)

- Look at the notes below.
- You will hear a man leaving a message for a colleague about another company's press conference.

NOTES ON WEBSTER'S PRESS CONFERENCE

Webster intends to:

- increase number of (5) .... in next few years.

- create position of (6) .... under Marketing Director.

- centralise the system for (7) ....

- introduce (8) ....

Conversation Three

(Questions 9–12)

- Look at the notes below.
- You will hear a man telephoning a colleague about a building he has seen.

ENTERPRISE BUSINESS COLLEGE

Notes about 15 Lemmington Road

Good points

- Not necessary to (9) .... it.

- Lower (10) .... than many other buildings for rent.

- It's in the suburbs, so the (11) .... tax is lower.

But . . .
- further from HQ.
- In the (12) ...., it may not be spacious enough.

PART TWO

Questions 13–22

Section One

(Questions 13–17)

- You will hear five short recordings. Five speakers are talking about the use of technology in recruitment.
- For each recording, decide what recommendation the speaker makes concerning technology in recruitment.
- Write one letter (**A–H**) next to the number of the recording.
- Do not use any letter more than once.
- After you have listened once, replay the recordings.

13	**A** Advertise posts within the company as well as outside.
14	**B** Include detailed information about vacancies.
	C Make sure your website is kept up to date.
15	**D** Allocate suitable staff to maintain the website.
	E Re-design your non-web-based recruitment advertising.
16	**F** Use a range of technologies for contact with applicants.
17	**G** Ask potential applicants the most important questions first.
	H Maximise the opportunities offered by the internet.

Section Two

(Questions 18–22)

- You will hear another five recordings. Five speakers are talking about how to deal with complaints about goods.
- For each recording, decide what action the speaker is recommending.
- Write one letter (**A–H**) next to the number of the recording.
- Do not use any letter more than once.
- After you have listened once, replay the recordings.

18	**A** initiating an investigation
	B giving money back
19	**C** providing an identical replacement
	D offering an upgrade
20	**E** arranging free servicing
21	**F** organising free training
	G extending the warranty
22	**H** offering a credit note

PART THREE

Questions 23–30

- You will hear John Sergeant, a retail analyst, being interviewed about a chain of clothing stores called Sangra.
- For each question (**23–30**), mark one letter (**A**, **B** or **C**) for the correct answer.
- After you have listened once, replay the recording.

23 According to John Sergeant, why is Sangra doing so badly?

    A   It has fallen behind changes in the market.
    B   It is employing unsuitable designers.
    C   Its stores are unattractive buildings.

24 In John Sergeant's opinion, Sangra has failed to realise that

    A   some competitors are selling identical items more cheaply.
    B   middle-market customers have more money to spend.
    C   its current advertising campaign is unsuccessful.

25 John Sergeant blames Sangra's last Chief Executive for not

    A   following the advice of the Board.
    B   planning who should follow him.
    C   choosing a good time for expansion.

26 What difficulty is Sangra having in introducing the 'lifestyle' idea?

    A   Few of its stores are large enough.
    B   The staff oppose the change.
    C   The costs are too high.

27 John Sergeant expects Sangra to solve its problems by

    A   improving productivity.
    B   closing a number of stores.
    C   reducing its profit margins.

28 Sangra's management are starting to

    A   work more closely with the suppliers.
    B   do market research on the customers.
    C   encourage suggestions from the staff.

29   John Sergeant advises Sangra to

    A   concentrate on its new strategy.
    B   return to its previous strategy.
    C   develop an alternative strategy.

30   Sangra is about to change by

    A   opening large, new out-of-town stores.
    B   taking over a foreign company.
    C   starting to sell non-clothing products.

You now have 10 minutes to transfer your answers to your Answer Sheet.

SPEAKING   14 minutes

SAMPLE SPEAKING TASKS

PART ONE

In this part, the interlocutor asks questions to each of the candidates in turn. You have to give information about yourself and express personal opinions.

PART TWO

In this part of the test, you are asked to give a short talk on a business topic. You have to choose one of the topics from the three below and then talk for about one minute. You have one minute to prepare your ideas.

A: What is important when . . . ?

Planning a presentation
- Audience
- Equipment needed
-
-

B: What is important when . . . ?

Selecting an interpreter for a meeting with foreign clients
- Experience
- Reliability
-
-

C: What is important when . . . ?

Introducing a new product range onto the market
- Timing
- Advance publicity
-
-

PART THREE

In this part of the test, you are given a discussion topic. You have 30 seconds to look at the task prompt, an example of which is below, and then about three minutes to discuss the topic with your partner. After that, the examiner will ask you more questions related to the topic.

For **two** candidates

Selling old stock

The manufacturing company you work for needs to make space in its warehouse to stock its new products. The company would like to sell off end-of-range products at discounted prices.

You have been asked to make recommendations.

Discuss the situation together and decide:

- whether to offer the same discount on all products
- how customers could be informed of the discounts.

For **three** candidates

Selling old stock

The manufacturing company you work for needs to make space in its warehouse to stock its new products. The company would like to sell off end-of-range products at discounted prices.

You have been asked to make recommendations.

Discuss the situation together and decide:

- how much discount should be offered
- whether to offer the same discount on all products
- how customers could be informed of the discounts.

Follow-on questions

- Do you think discounts are a good way of selling old stock? (Why?/Why not?)

- In what other ways do you think companies can get rid of unwanted stock? (Why?)

- What do you think is the main disadvantage for a company of having too much stock in its warehouse?

- How do you think companies could plan their stock requirements more accurately?

- Why do you think it can be difficult to sell stock sometimes?

- How do you think discounting could affect a company's image? (Why?)

Test 2

READING   1 hour

PART ONE

Questions 1–7

- Look at the statements below and the advice to businesses on the opposite page about using other companies to run their IT services.
- Which section (**A, B, C** or **D**) does each statement (**1–7**) refer to?
- For each statement (**1–7**), mark one letter (**A, B, C** or **D**) on your Answer Sheet.
- You will need to use some of these letters more than once.

Example:

0   outsourced processes not being entirely separate from the rest of the business

---

1   the need to teach skills to employees working on the outsourced process

2   remembering the initial reason for setting up the outsourced project

3   the need to draw up agreements that set out how integration is to be achieved

4   addressing the issue of staff who work on the outsourced process being at a distant site

5   the importance of making someone responsible for the integration process

6   staff on the outsourced project familiarising themselves with various details of the business

7   problems being associated with an alternative to outsourcing

When a business decides to outsource its IT services, it needs to consider the question of integration. Four experts give their views.

A

Gianluca Tramcere, Silica Systems
An outsourced IT service is never a fully independent entity. It is tied to the home company's previous and continuing systems of working. But despite the added responsibility of managing new ways of working, many businesses ignore the integration process. They fail to establish contracts that define the ways in which the two companies will work alongside one another, and focus solely on the technological aspects of service delivery.

B

Kevin Rayner, Domola
Businesses need to build integration competency centres dedicated to managing the integration effort. It is critical to have an individual in charge to check that the external and internal business operations work together. Although companies often think of outsourcing as a way of getting rid of people and assets, they need to remember that, at the same time, outsourcing involves gaining people. Because there is a new operation being carried out in a different way outside of the home business, this creates a training element.

C

Clayton Locke, Digital Solutions
Communication is the key to success, and outsourcing to other regions or countries can lead to a range of problems. For any such initiative, it is necessary to create a team where there is good, open communication and a clear understanding of objectives and incentives. Bringing people to the home location from the outsourced centre is necessary, since it can aid understanding of the complexities of the existing system. To integrate efficiently, outsourcing personnel have to talk to the home company's executives and users to understand their experiences.

D

Kim Noon, J G Tech
One way to avoid the difficulties of integration is to create a joint-venture company with the outsourcer. Thus, a company can swap its assets for a share of the profits. Yet joint ventures bring potential troubles, and companies should be careful not to lose sight of the original rationale for outsourcing: to gain cost efficiencies and quality of service in an area that for some reason could not be carried out entirely in-house. The complexities and costs of a joint-venture initiative should not be underestimated.

PART TWO

Questions 8–12

- Read the article below about the changing role of human resources departments.
- Choose the best sentence from the opposite page to fill each of the gaps.
- For each gap (**8–12**), mark one letter (**A–G**) on your Answer Sheet.
- Do not use any letter more than once.
- There is an example at the beginning (**0**).

The best person for the job

Employees can make a business succeed or fail, so the people who choose them have a vital role to play

Employees are a company's new ideas, its public face and its main asset. Hiring the right people is therefore a significant factor in a company's success. (**0**) .....G....... If the human resources department makes mistakes with hiring, keeping and dismissing staff, a business can disappear overnight. Many companies now realise that recruiting the best recruiters is the key to success.

Sarah Choi, Head of HR at Enco plc, believes that thinking commercially is a key quality in HR. 'Every decision an HR manager makes needs to be relevant to advancing the business. (**8**) .... That's no longer the case. HR managers have to think more strategically these days. They continually need to think about the impact of their decisions on the bottom line. (**9**) .... For example, a chief executive will expect the HR department to advise on everything from the headcount to whether to proceed with an acquisition.'

Why do people go into HR in the first place? Choi has a ready answer. 'I think most people in the profession are attracted by a long-term goal. (**10**) .... Nothing happens in the company which isn't affected by or doesn't impact on its employees, so the HR department is a crucial part of any business.'

Not all operational managers agree. An informal survey of attitudes to HR departments that was carried out last year by a leading business journal received comments such as 'What do they actually contribute?' (**11**) .... As Choi points out, salaries have never been higher and, in addition, HR managers often receive substantial annual bonuses.

Despite the financial rewards, HR managers often feel undervalued, and this is a major reason for many leaving their jobs. (**12**) .... However, a lack of training and development is a more significant factor. 'These days, good professional development opportunities are considered an essential part of an attractive package,' Choi explains.

Example:

A But rising levels of remuneration demonstrate that the profession's growing importance is widely recognised.

B At one time, a professional qualification was required in order to progress to the top of HR.

C Other departments and senior executives used to see HR managers as having a purely administrative role.

D Since it's one of the few areas where you can see the whole operation, it can lead to an influential role on the board.

E Being seen as someone who just ticks off other people's leave and sick days does not help build a sense of loyalty.

F They therefore need to be competent in many aspects of a company's operations.

G On the other hand, recruiting the wrong staff can lead to disaster.

PART THREE

Questions 13–18

- Read the article below about a technology company and the questions on the opposite page.
- For each question (**13–18**), mark one letter (**A**, **B**, **C** or **D**) on your Answer Sheet.

Critical Path

When David Hayden realised his company was heading for trouble, he took drastic measures to get it back on track

David Hayden founded his company, Critical Path, an email provider, in 1997 to take advantage of the boom in email traffic. Critical Path became a public company two years later, and Hayden took the opportunity to step down from his executive position in order to work on personal projects. At the same time, he agreed to stay with the company as Chairman, but the business was put in the hands of new managers by its investors. With sector-leading products and an expanding market, the company seemed to be on the up and up. However, by early 2001, it was in trouble. Shares that had been worth $26 in 1999, when they were first sold, were down to a mere 24 cents.

Called in by a panicking board, Hayden found himself back in charge as Executive Chairman, trying desperately to rescue what he could. The 1,100 staff had lost confidence in the company and did not know what was going to happen to them. And, as Hayden discovered, the management team was incompetent. 'Those guys didn't understand the product or the sector,' says Hayden. 'The heads of department didn't communicate and they didn't lead.' But what was worse, Critical Path had lost the goodwill of its investors.

Hayden knew that bringing the figures under control would be a vital step in the company's turnaround. 'You've got to sort out the finances. For me, that meant getting back the goodwill of the investors. That was tough, after what had happened. But although they were angry with the company, they didn't have bad feelings about me. I told them that I knew I could get the company on its feet again.' He was authorised to make whatever changes were required, and his first act was to find people within the company he could trust and put them in charge.

The next thing Hayden had to tackle was morale. 'Everyone left the office at five on the dot – they couldn't get away quickly enough. To get the buzz back and win the staff over, I had to prove my own commitment and put in the extra hours with them.' In return, it was assumed that nobody would ask for overtime pay until the company was on its feet again. Contrary to normal practice, Hayden was reluctant to lay people off, and apart from not replacing people as they reached retirement age, he left the workforce largely unchanged, although he did identify key people throughout the company who were given more responsibility.

But, as Hayden insists, before a company reaches such a crisis, there are warning signs that any financial director or accountant should take note of. 'A business that has an unrealistic pricing policy or has to negotiate extended credit with its suppliers is in trouble,' is his message. 'Or if you often have to apply for your overdraft limit to be raised or have trouble paying tax on time, something needs to be done.'

By 2003, the company was healthy again, with reasonably stable finances and a modest but steady share price of $1.60. 'One thing that helped save us was that our technology worked,' says Hayden. 'With 20 million email accounts, we never lost a single major client because the product kept on working.' With ideas for a fresh venture demanding his attention elsewhere, Hayden has moved on. 'It was time to go,' he says. 'I'm not a turnaround specialist. I prefer start-ups.'

13   What event coincided with Critical Path becoming a public company?

    A   Hayden became the Executive Director of Critical Path.
    B   Investors hired a replacement team to run Critical Path.
    C   Critical Path launched a successful new product on the market.
    D   Critical Path was floated on the Stock Exchange at 24 cents per share.

14   Which of the following situations did Hayden face at Critical Path in 2001?

    A   The employees were worried about job security.
    B   The investors were calling for changes to the company structure.
    C   The management was misleading the staff about the company's position.
    D   The board of directors did not realise the scale of the company's problems.

15   One reason Hayden was able to turn Critical Path around was that

    A   he managed to find new investors.
    B   the financial situation was not as bad as he had thought.
    C   he had built up a good relationship with the management team.
    D   he was given the support that he needed.

16   What was Hayden's policy regarding the staff of Critical Path?

    A   He paid overtime to everybody who worked outside office hours.
    B   He reduced the workforce by operating an early retirement scheme.
    C   He gave key staff the opportunity to help him set goals for the company.
    D   He restored motivation by showing willingness to work alongside staff.

17   According to Hayden, what could indicate that a business is in trouble?

    A   problems keeping accounts up to date
    B   suppliers refusing to offer new credit terms
    C   a frequent need to increase the amount borrowed
    D   difficulties in getting payment from customers on time

18   Hayden left Critical Path after he had rescued the company because

    A   he wanted to develop the technology for a new internet service.
    B   he wanted to concentrate on founding a new enterprise.
    C   he had been offered a job with a major internet company.
    D   he decided to go into partnership with a major client.

PART FOUR

Questions 19–33

- Read the news item below about a company that runs health and fitness clubs.
- Choose the best word to fill each gap from **A**, **B**, **C** or **D** on the opposite page.
- For each question (**19–33**), mark one letter (**A**, **B**, **C** or **D**) on your Answer Sheet.
- There is an example at the beginning (**0**).

Fighting Fit

Fine Fitness, the health and fitness club operator, (**0**) ......*D*..... an impressive set of results yesterday. (**19**) .... a 38-per-cent jump in annual pre-tax profits, the company claimed that it had (**20**) .... none of the problems (**21**) .... last week by its rival, Top Fit. According to Samantha Collier, the chief executive, Fine Fitness (**22**) .... strong and is on (**23**) .... to reach its target of 100 clubs within three years, its strategy unaffected by the apparent (**24**) .... down of the economy.

The company opened 12 new clubs in the past year, (**25**) .... its total to 51. They have (**26**) .... to be highly successful, with people joining in large numbers, especially in the 25-to-40 age range. Even the more (**27**) .... clubs are still seeing sales growth, along with rising retention (**28**) .... of more than 70 per cent. This can be seen as clear (**29**) .... of the appeal of Fine Fitness.

Ms Collier admitted that as there were (**30**) .... too many companies competing with one another, there would almost certainly be (**31**) .... in the health-and-fitness-club sector of the market. She predicted that, within a relatively short time, there might be only about three major companies still in (**32**) .... However, she declined to say which these were likely to be.

Profits rose by £6.3 million, although there was a fall in gross margins from 31 per cent to 28.6 per cent because of higher insurance premiums, extra management costs and start-up expenses for the company's new (**33**) .... in Spain.

Example:

| A stated | B expressed | C said | D announced |

	A	B	C	D
0	☐	☐	☐	▬

19	**A** Stating	**B** Reporting	**C** Remarking	**D** Informing
20	**A** taken	**B** felt	**C** experienced	**D** caught
21	**A** released	**B** issued	**C** opened	**D** revealed
22	**A** stays	**B** remains	**C** maintains	**D** keeps
23	**A** track	**B** direction	**C** way	**D** line
24	**A** falling	**B** breaking	**C** cutting	**D** slowing
25	**A** bringing	**B** putting	**C** getting	**D** mounting
26	**A** shown	**B** resulted	**C** proved	**D** demonstrated
27	**A** installed	**B** formed	**C** established	**D** confirmed
28	**A** rates	**B** standards	**C** proportions	**D** volumes
29	**A** witness	**B** sign	**C** display	**D** evidence
30	**A** purely	**B** merely	**C** simply	**D** barely
31	**A** union	**B** consolidation	**C** alliance	**D** combination
32	**A** trade	**B** office	**C** commerce	**D** business
33	**A** trial	**B** venture	**C** proposal	**D** speculation

PART FIVE

Questions 34–45

- Read the article below about a manufacturing company called Lebrun.
- In most of the lines (**34–45**), there is one extra word. It either is grammatically incorrect or does not fit in with the meaning of the text. Some lines, however, are correct.
- If a line is correct, write **CORRECT** on your Answer Sheet.
- If there is an extra word in the line, write **the extra word** in CAPITAL LETTERS on your Answer Sheet.
- The exercise begins with two examples (**0** and **00**).

Examples:	**0**	A	S						
	00	C	O	R	R	E	C	T	

Lebrun Steel Facing up to Tough Times

0 After 98 years of trading, the steel manufacturer Lebrun knows from experience as how

00 difficult fluctuations in the economic cycle can be for suppliers such as themselves.

34 Since many of the nation's largest production companies which are its customers,

35 Lebrun is adversely affected by any change for the worse in the economy. Yet Lebrun

36 has managed to keep on sales steady (in the region of approximately $2.5 billion)

37 and has recorded only one annual loss during the difficulties of the past five

38 years, but despite the effects of the ongoing industrial slowdown. James Griffith,

39 president of Lebrun, now has the task of turning up survival into growth, and

40 his strategy is already becoming clear to those industry observers. In February of

41 this year, the company acquired Bronson plc, additionally a one-time competitor.

42 This merger will greatly expand the size of both Lebrun's labour force, and

43 Griffith estimates it will boost its revenue by nearly 50%, while too increasing

44 the number of plants and R&D centres in much a similar way. Griffith is

45 optimistic that while the steel industry is about to pull out of recession, and

he wants Lebrun to be ready for this.

WRITING 45 minutes

PART ONE

- The software company you work for has decided to introduce identity cards for certain staff in your department.
- Write an **email** to all staff in your department:
  - saying which staff will need identity cards
  - explaining why the identity cards are needed
  - informing staff how to get a card.
- Write **40–50** words.

PART TWO

- The number of staff leaving Parkside, one of your company's retail stores, is high compared to another of its stores. Your line manager has asked you to write a report about the situation.
- Look at the information below, on which you have already made some handwritten notes.
- Then, using **all** your handwritten notes, write your **report**.
- Write **120–140** words.

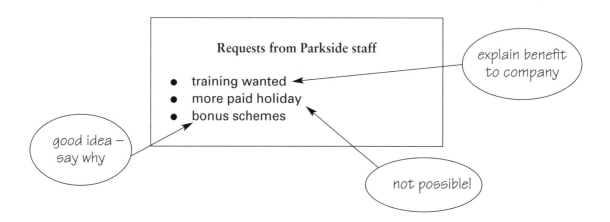

LISTENING   40 minutes (including
10 minutes' transfer time)

PART ONE

Questions 1–12

- You will hear three telephone conversations or messages.
- Write **one** or **two** words or a number in the numbered spaces on the notes or forms below.
- After you have listened once, replay each recording.

Conversation One

(Questions 1–4)

- Look at the note below.
- You will hear a man clarifying some information about a balance sheet.

Message for Bill

Tom rang re queries on balance sheet for (1) ....

Figures in column A deal with (2) .... liabilities.

Figures for assets include (3) .... assets only.

Section 4 figures indicate (4) .... over last two years.

Conversation Two

(Questions 5–8)

- Look at the notes below.
- You will hear a man leaving a voicemail message about a negotiating problem.

ANSWERPHONE MESSAGE

Kristoff called from Australia.

Client now unhappy about proposed date for finishing the
(5) …................................. .

Also wants to include (6) …................................ which could cost us
3% per week.

To finish on time, we would need extra (7) …................................
workers from start of project.

Our company will be given (8) …................................ for next project if
we complete on time.

Conversation Three

(Questions 9–12)

- Look at the notes below.
- You will hear a woman telephoning a colleague about a new project.

E-commerce Website Project

Notes

Team: we need to recruit an (9) ....
to solve programming problems.

Report: needed by end of week. Should include:

- some indication of (10)
  .... of project

- details of (11) ....
  that will be needed

- clear statement of the (12) ....
  of project.

PART TWO

Questions 13–22

Section One

(Questions 13–17)

- You will hear five short recordings.
- For each recording, decide which aspect of conducting interviews each speaker considers particularly important.
- Write one letter (**A–H**) next to the number of the recording.
- Do not use any letter more than once.
- After you have listened once, replay the recordings.

13 ....

14 ....

15 ....

16 ....

17 ....

A	asking the applicant some hard questions
B	including a practical task in the interview
C	helping the applicant to relax
D	giving the interviewee a chance to ask questions
E	discussing references with the interviewee
F	judging how the applicant would behave at work
G	checking the relevance of the applicant's experience
H	having several interviewers on the panel

Section Two

(Questions 18–22)

- You will hear another five recordings. Five speakers are talking about problems with a project.
- For each recording, decide what the problem was.
- Write one letter (**A–H**) next to the number of the recording.
- Do not use any letter more than once.
- After you have listened once, replay the recordings.

18 ....

19 ....

20 ....

21 ....

22 ....

A	Staff were unhappy about working overtime.
B	The budget was inadequate.
C	The wrong equipment was delivered.
D	The equipment was unreliable.
E	The customer changed the specifications.
F	Staff lacked relevant skills.
G	The supplier went bankrupt.
H	Too few staff were recruited

PART THREE

Questions 23–30

- You will hear a radio reporter talking about difficulties faced by the new Chief Executive of Healthway plc, a chain of health and beauty stores.
- For each question (**23–30**), mark one letter (**A**, **B** or **C**) for the correct answer.
- After you have listened once, replay the recording.

23 The Chief Executive is in a difficult position because Healthway plc is

    A   becoming less popular with the general public.

    B   failing to attract new shareholders.

    C   suffering from a history of static sales.

24 What form of competition is a threat to Healthway plc?

    A   the growth of internet shopping

    B   supermarkets undercutting its prices

    C   other health and beauty chains opening stores

25 How does Healthway plc differ from Robert Henlow's previous employer?

    A   Most senior staff have been promoted internally.

    B   Senior staff are generally appointed from outside.

    C   It has a high turnover of senior staff.

26 The reporter's criticism of Charles Hamilton's financial strategy is that the company

    A   under-invested in its systems.

    B   failed to grow through takeovers.

    C   paid too little attention to its share price.

27 With regard to the beauty treatment centres, Charles Hamilton is criticised for

    A   closing a chain which had the potential for making a profit.

    B   over-investing in the centres at the expense of the core activity.

    C   starting a new concept that was unlikely to succeed.

28 What mistake did Charles Hamilton make with regard to staff?

    A   failing to ensure that the need for reorganisation was understood

    B   concentrating redundancies in the wrong parts of the company

    C   getting rid of too many people with essential skills

29 What does the consultants' report recommend?

    A   reducing the total number of stores

    B   increasing the average size of the stores

    C   leaving staff numbers unchanged

30 Why is Robert Henlow's new position a personal challenge for him?

    A   He has never worked in a company with such serious problems.

    B   It is his first appointment as Chief Executive of a large company.

    C   He is unfamiliar with the sector in which Healthway operates.

You now have 10 minutes to transfer your answers to your Answer Sheet.

SPEAKING   14 minutes

SAMPLE SPEAKING TASKS

PART ONE

In this part, the interlocutor asks questions to each of the candidates in turn. You have to give information about yourself and express personal opinions.

PART TWO

In this part of the test, you are asked to give a short talk on a business topic. You have to choose one of the topics from the three below and then talk for about one minute. You have one minute to prepare your ideas.

A: What is important when . . .?

Aiming to improve career prospects
- Reading business articles
- Learning a foreign language
-
-

B: What is important when . . . ?

Deciding how to transport goods
- Destination
- Speed
-
-

C: What is important when . . . ?

Purchasing new machinery
- Level of automation
- Maintenance requirement
-
-

PART THREE

In this part of the test, you are given a discussion topic. You have 30 seconds to look at the task prompt, an example of which is below, and then about three minutes to discuss the topic with your partner. After that, the examiner will ask you more questions related to the topic.

For **two** candidates

Promoting a new model

The car manufacturer you work for plans to produce a new model and to target consumers between 18 and 25 years old.

You have been asked to make suggestions for promoting the car.

Discuss the situation together and decide:

- which features of a car might be important to the target group
- how an advertising campaign could present the car.

For **three** candidates

Promoting a new model

The car manufacturer you work for plans to produce a new model and to target consumers between 18 and 25 years old.

You have been asked to make suggestions for promoting the car.

Discuss the situation together, and decide:

- which features of a car might be important to the target group
- how an advertising campaign could present the car
- where you could advertise the car.

Follow-on questions

- If you were buying a car, which features would most influence you? (Why?)

- Apart from the age of target consumers, what might influence companies when pricing new products? (Why?)

- How easily influenced do you think consumers are by advertising campaigns? (Why?/Why not?)

- Why might it be necessary for companies to introduce new products regularly?

- Do you think timing is important when launching new products? (Why?/Why not?)

- Why do you think companies decide to stop making a product?

Test 3

READING   1 hour

PART ONE

Questions 1–7

- Look at the statements below and the article about pricing on the opposite page.
- Which section (**A**, **B**, **C** or **D**) does each statement (**1–7**) refer to?
- For each statement (**1–7**), mark one letter (**A**, **B**, **C** or **D**) on your Answer Sheet.
- You will need to use some of these letters more than once.

Example:

0   the price depending on the product features chosen by the customer

---

1   the failure of a company to set its prices appropriately

2   a context that makes it difficult to increase prices

3   the consequences of companies trying to conceal their approach to pricing

4   the means by which a company ensured precision in the prices it offered

5   the fact that companies can learn about the effects of a price reduction

6   the first sector to price products according to how much customers were prepared to spend

7   the widespread use of rough guidelines to determine prices

Getting the price right

A Chief executives need to pay more attention to pricing, according to Roberto Lippi of the Apex Group, a consultancy that offers advice on pricing strategy. He accepts that low inflation figures in many industrialised countries makes raising prices tough, but argues that this should not necessarily deter companies. He gives the example of the airlines, which, with their minimum stay requirements and massive premiums for flexibility, led the way in sorting customers into categories, based on their willingness to pay.

B The key to pricing is to avoid alienating customers. As Lippi points out, once a bad price has been established, it can be very difficult to turn the situation around. He gives the example of a consumer goods company that went bankrupt largely because it did not price its digital cameras properly. In contrast, he cites the case of a Swiss drug company that introduced software for every sales representative's laptop, enabling them to provide consistent and accurate price quotes. To help staff with this innovation, the company also created a new post of director of pricing strategy.

C Many of today's managers have the benefit of modern technology to help them with pricing. Supermarket chains, for example, can easily track customers' 'elasticity' – how their buying habits change in response to a price rise or a discount. But although a company can now measure this sort of thing in a more sophisticated way, following basic rules is still the most common way of setting prices. Most bosses still worry more about their costs than the prices they charge; one recent survey found that they spend as little as 2% of their time on pricing.

D One popular approach to pricing is illustrated by the car companies that charge extra for product add-ons such as electric windows, instead of offering them as part of the standard price. Although many customers are prepared to pay extra, Lippi recommends that companies make sure that price differences reflect real differences in the product, either in quality or in the extra service on offer. The worst approach is to try to keep the pricing structure secret from customers. Nowadays, that is more likely to lead to lost contracts than large profits.

PART TWO

Questions 8–12

- Read the article below about the role of executive recruitment agencies.
- Choose the best sentence from the opposite page to fill each of the gaps.
- For each gap (**8–12**), mark one letter (**A–G**) on your Answer Sheet.
- Do not use any letter more than once.
- There is an example at the beginning (**0**).

Issues in the recruitment world

In the competitive world of investment banking, good senior executives are not easy to find. So what should the industry's hard-pressed directors do when they need to find senior staff? Increasingly, they decide to call in the headhunters. These are busy and profitable times for the recruitment agencies that dominate the world of executive search and selection.

(0) .....G..... They needed new people to revitalise their operations, and the result has been a boom in the recruitment market. Pinnacle, a leading recruitment agency, has helped various UK investment banks to rebuild their entire senior management teams. It is hard to overstate the significance of this. **(8)** ....

But now everything has changed, and Pinnacle is not the only major player in the field. Some analysts believe that rival recruitment specialists ALT Associates has a larger share of the market. However, there is little doubt that over its 13-year history, Pinnacle and its chairman, Matthew Edwards, have built up an impressive reputation.

Edwards estimates that his company controls between 10 and 15 per cent of the headhunting market for senior investment banking jobs in the UK. **(9)** .... Rather, it is the high-calibre jobs and people that Pinnacle deals with that define the company's success. For example, the company was recently commissioned to find a new chairman for NBS Bank, a vacancy that was one of the most talked about in the banking world.

Most HR directors recognise that headhunters such as Pinnacle play a valuable role in the recruitment process. **(10)** .... Some are concerned that a few companies, including Pinnacle, have too much power over high-level recruitment. **(11)** .... As Tim Davidson, HR Director at Cawfield Bank, explains, 'They can be kingmakers. These are the people who decide who gets a future and who doesn't. If Edwards forms a view about an individual, it can affect their ability to get a particular job. That view could just have been formed on a bad day.' **(12)** .... Final decisions in the selection process are always taken by his clients, he says, whoever they are.

The role of headhunters should not be exaggerated. Many companies never use them. But as top executives are hard to find, there will always be a role for people like Matthew Edwards.

Example:

A   Although others may put it lower, it is important to remember that the company's reputation is not based on market share alone.

B   Their chief worry is that the headhunters can now make or break managerial careers.

C   According to Edwards, this is a further indication that the way Pinnacle searches for a candidate tends to favour a certain type of manager.

D   But this acceptance does not mean they are universally happy, either with the state of the market or with Pinnacle's role within it.

E   Until a few years ago, even the biggest companies were unlikely to use headhunters to fill more than one or two jobs a year.

F   Edwards objects to this suggestion, claiming that all he does is find candidates and encourage them to apply for a particular post.

G   A number of big investment banks recently decided to make changes to their management boards after disappointing end-of-year results.

PART THREE

Questions 13–18

- Read the advice below about producing a company brochure and the questions on the opposite page.
- For each question (**13–18**), mark one letter (**A**, **B**, **C** or **D**) on your Answer Sheet.

THE ART OF PERSUASION

'Let me send you our brochure' is probably the most commonly used phrase in business. But all too often, it can spell the end of a customer enquiry because many brochures appear to be produced not to clarify and to excite but to confuse. So what goes wrong and how can it be put right? Too often, businesses fail to ask themselves critical questions like, 'Who will the brochure be sent to?' 'What do we want to achieve with it?' The truth is that a brochure has usually been produced for no other reason than that the competition has one.

However, with a little research, it often transpires that what the client wants is a mixture: part mail shot, part glossy corporate brochure and part product catalogue – a combination rarely found. Having said that, the budget is likely to be finite. There may not be enough money to meet all three marketing needs, so the first task is to plan the brochure, taking into account the most significant of these. The other requirements will have to be met in a different way. After all, introducing the company's product range to new customers by mail is a different task from selling a new season's collection to existing customers.

The second task is to get the content right. In 95 per cent of cases, a company will hire a designer to oversee the layout, so the final product looks stylish, interesting and professional; but they don't get a copywriter or someone with the right expertise to produce the text, or at least tidy it up – and this shows. A bigger failing is to produce a brochure that is not customer focused. Your brochure should cover areas of interest to the customer, concentrating on the benefits of buying from you.

Instead, thousands of brochures start with a history lesson, 'Founded in 1987, we have been selling our products . . .'. I can assure you that customers are never going to say to themselves, 'They've been around for 20 years – I'll buy from them.' It's not how long you've been in business that counts, it's what you've done in that time. The important point to get across at the beginning is that you have a good track record. Once this has been established, the rest of the brochure should aim to convince customers that your products are the best on the market.

It is helpful with content to get inside the customer's head. If your audience is young and trendy, be creative and colourful. As always, create a list of the benefits that potential customers would gain from doing business with you, for example, product quality, breadth of range, expertise of staff and so on. But remember that it is not enough just to state these; in order to persuade, they need to be spelt out. One possibility is to quote recommendations from existing customers. This also makes the brochure personal to you, rather than it simply being a set of suppliers' photographs with your name on the front.

At the design stage, there are many production features that can distinguish your brochure from the run of the mill. You may *line 67* think that things like cutouts or pop-ups will do this for you and thus make you stand out, or you may think they just look like designer whims that add cost. Go through all the options in detail. One of them might be that all-important magical ingredient.

13 What point does the writer make about brochures in the first paragraph?

    A   Customer expectations of them are too high.
    B   They ought to be more straightforward in design.
    C   Insufficient thought tends to go into producing them.
    D   Companies should ensure they use them more widely.

14 The writer's advice to companies in the second paragraph is to

    A   produce a brochure to advertise new product lines.
    B   use a brochure to extend the customer base.
    C   accept that a brochure cannot fulfil every objective.
    D   aim to get a bigger budget allocation for producing brochures.

15 In the third paragraph, which of the following does the writer say would improve the majority of brochures?

    A   better language and expression
    B   better overall appearance
    C   more up-to-date content
    D   more product information

16 In the introduction to a brochure, the writer advises companies to focus on

    A   their understanding of the business environment.
    B   the range of products they offer.
    C   their unique market position.
    D   the reputation they have built up.

17 When discussing brochure content in the fifth paragraph, the writer reminds companies to

    A   consider old customers as well as new ones.
    B   provide support for the claims they make.
    C   avoid using their own photographs.
    D   include details of quality certification.

18 What does 'run of the mill' in line 67 mean?

    A   eye-catching
    B   complicated
    C   stylish
    D   ordinary

PART FOUR

Questions 19–33

- Read the article below about online exchanges, a type of internet business.
- Choose the best word or phrase to fill each gap from **A**, **B**, **C** or **D** on the opposite page.
- For each question (**19–33**), mark one letter (**A**, **B**, **C** or **D**) on your Answer Sheet.
- There is an example at the beginning (**0**).

Online exchanges?

*Online exchanges have emerged as some of the internet's best
businesses – but also as some of the worst*

So the internet hasn't revolutionised the (**0**) .....A.... most of us buy petrol, or watch movies. But there is one thing the internet does very well. It can bring together (**19**) .... dispersed buyers and sellers to create active, efficient markets where none (**20**) .... before. This facility has (**21**) .... to the emergence of online exchanges: retail businesses with none of the usual traders' risks – no merchandise, no storefronts – and with nothing to do but take a (**22**) .... of each transaction that takes place on the site.

This may sound straightforward, but some high-profile online exchanges have (**23**) .... out to be major embarrassments. One company, which tried to establish a central marketplace on the internet for auto parts, has invested, in (**24**) .... , a massive $250m and is (**25**) .... to stay in business. Another businessman, who facilitated online trading in business equipment and supplies, (**26**) .... after he had lost $280m.

So what does a company need in order to be successful? You could call it good 'market architecture' – a structure that (**27**) .... the right business plan and top technology with good timing and the (**28**) .... of both buyers and sellers.

Mike Pham's company, eStream, is an excellent example of one business that met these (**29**) .... Back in 1996, when Pham was looking for a loan, he didn't like filling in the same form every time he (**30**) .... to a new lender. That got him thinking. Why not (**31**) .... prospective borrowers to complete a standard form and circulate that to a number of lenders, who would then make an offer to the borrower, in (**32**) .... with each other?

Pham's company is doing well. Last year, eStream (**33**) .... more than 1.5 million loans on behalf of 170 lenders.

Example:

	A way	B style	C method	D manner

```
┌─────┬─────────────────────┐
│  0  │  A    B    C    D    │
│     │  ▄▄   ▭    ▭    ▭    │
└─────┴─────────────────────┘
```

#	A	B	C	D
19	A largely	B deeply	C mainly	D widely
20	A existed	B occurred	C happened	D developed
21	A led	B brought	C caused	D resulted
22	A number	B percentage	C division	D quantity
23	A pulled	B made	C turned	D carried
24	A sum	B total	C amount	D figure
25	A applying	B exerting	C struggling	D forcing
26	A left out	B gave up	C drew back	D ran down
27	A adds	B connects	C combines	D links
28	A confidence	B security	C certainty	D promise
29	A necessities	B propositions	C measures	D criteria
30	A requested	B asked	C applied	D demanded
31	A attract	B invite	C suggest	D recommend
32	A contrast	B conflict	C challenge	D competition
33	A performed	B dealt	C handled	D treated

PART FIVE

Questions 34–45

- Read the extract below from a company report.
- In most of the lines (**34–45**), there is one extra word. It is either grammatically incorrect or does not fit in with the meaning of the text. Some lines, however, are correct.
- If a line is correct, write **CORRECT** on your Answer Sheet.
- If there is an extra word in the line, write **the extra word** in CAPITAL LETTERS on your Answer Sheet.
- The exercise begins with two examples (**0** and **00**).

Examples:	**0**	C	O	R	R	E	C	T		
	00	M	O	S	T					

Summary of annual progress

0 I am pleased to report another year of progress by the company. This

00 performance has been achieved in the most toughest market conditions we have

34 seen for many years yet. It reflects the effort over the past five years that has

35 gone into transforming of our company into a highly competitive world-class

36 business. Since 2002, we have managed to improve almost double our profits, and this

37 increase in profitability has been placed us at the top of the global glass industry.

38 We have managed to succeed this in difficult trading conditions for a number of

39 reasons, the most important of which has been from our ability to stay ahead

40 of our competitors. We have refused to allow stand still and have continued to bring

41 out a number of new products, most of which are already on the sale in our key

42 markets. All this goes to confirm that the company's position as the recognised

43 industry leader in technical innovation. We realise that there is still much more to

44 be done, but we believe that we know precisely what extra this is and we have

45 already put into place organisational and technical changes to bring this about.

WRITING   45 minutes

PART ONE

- You work for a large company. You are going to be transferred to another department within your company.
- Write an **email** to all staff:
  - telling them which department you are moving to
  - saying when you will be moving department
  - explaining what your new responsibilities will be.
- Write **40–50** words.

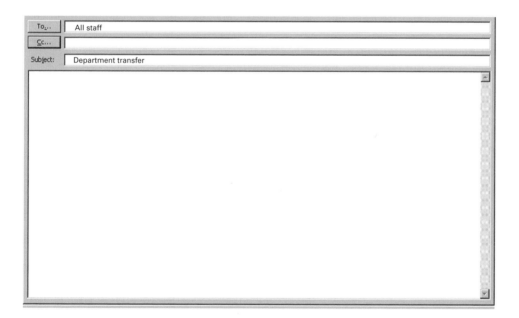

PART TWO

- You are a regional manager for a retail company. Your line manager at head office would like a report about three of the stores in your region, including a recommendation to close one of them.
- Look at the information below, on which you have already made some handwritten notes.
- Then, using **all** your handwritten notes, write your **report**.
- Write **120–140** words.

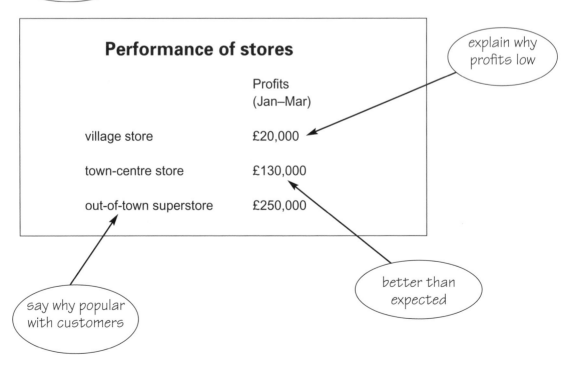

In order to reduce costs, we are considering closing one of the stores in your region. Which store is performing badly and should be closed? Is there a new service we could offer to attract more customers to the stores we keep open?

suggest closing village store

suggest something

Performance of stores

	Profits (Jan–Mar)
village store	£20,000
town-centre store	£130,000
out-of-town superstore	£250,000

explain why profits low

say why popular with customers

better than expected

LISTENING   40 minutes (including 10 minutes' transfer time)

PART ONE

Questions 1–12

- You will hear three telephone conversations or messages.
- Write **one** or **two** words or a number in the numbered spaces on the notes or forms below.
- After you have listened once, replay each recording.

Conversation One

(Questions 1–4)

- Look at the notes below.
- You will hear a phone conversation between a manager and his PA.

Fax to Barry

Document entitled (1) ....

Saved in (2) .... folder

No need to include (3) ....

Fax to (4) ....

Conversation Two

(Questions 5–8)

- Look at the notes below.
- You will hear two colleagues discussing an additional location for their business.

Discussion Notes

Subject: Location of (**5**) ....

Business park more convenient for (**6**) ....

According to our (**7**) .... , customers will go to business park.

If we rent space in business park, company will be able to claim (**8**) ....

Conversation Three

(Questions 9–12)

- Look at the note below.
- You will hear a woman leaving a message about where to hold a meeting.

Message

From: Emily Parker

She has found appropriate venue for the

(9) .... meeting.

The (10) .... at the Carlton

Hotel is available on 25/10.

The Carlton can provide a (11) ....

for free.

Call the (12) .... Manager on

357209 to book.

PART TWO

Questions 13–22

Section One

(Questions 13–17)

- You will hear five short recordings. Five speakers are talking about delegating at work.
- For each recording, decide what advice the speaker gives about delegating at work.
- Write one letter (**A–H**) next to the number of the recording.
- Do not use any letter more than once.
- After you have listened once, replay the recordings.

13	....
14	....
15	....
16	....
17	....

A	Make sure you delegate for the right reasons.
B	Don't delegate to very new staff.
C	Discuss fully what problems might arise.
D	Set up a support network for staff.
E	Give people freedom to act for themselves.
F	Provide staff with feedback during tasks.
G	Review performance when tasks are completed.
H	Don't be discouraged by a lack of success.

Section Two

(Questions 18–22)

- You will hear another five recordings. Five speakers are talking about the reason for the success of their company's most recent TV advertising campaign.
- For each recording, decide what reason the speaker gives for the success of the campaign.
- Write one letter (**A–H**) next to the number of the recording.
- Do not use any letter more than once.
- After you have listened once, replay the recordings.

18	....
19	....
20	....
21	....
22	....

A	More money than usual was allocated to the campaign.
B	A new production company was used for the commercial.
C	The advice of consultants was acted upon.
D	A different type of customer was attracted.
E	A competitor's problem benefited the company.
F	The campaign was accompanied by mail-shot samples.
G	More comprehensive research was done.
H	A new team took responsibility for the project.

PART THREE

Questions 23–30

- You will hear a radio interview with a businessman called Brett Porter, who developed a product called Rainaway, a type of waterproof map.
- For each question (**23–30**), mark one letter (**A**, **B** or **C**) for the correct answer.
- After you have listened once, replay the recording.

23   Why did Brett decide to try to produce the Rainaway map?

   A   He was assured that it was better than existing products of that type.
   B   He could see a way of manufacturing it reasonably cheaply.
   C   He was unable to buy anything similar himself.

24   When he started to develop Rainaway, Brett was confident of his knowledge of

   A   target customers.
   B   distribution methods.
   C   pricing strategies.

25   What helped Brett's business to grow?

   A   a low-interest loan from a commercial bank
   B   an informal discussion with a business adviser
   C   free software from a firm called Croner Consulting

26   What problem was there with the trial production of Rainaway?

   A   the small size of the printed product
   B   the low quality of the print materials
   C   the slow printing process used

27   What problem did Brett have with printing companies?

   A   They were unwilling to make a long-lasting product.
   B   They misunderstood his business idea.
   C   They wanted to charge more for a high-risk project.

28   Brett realises that Herne Publishing might try to

   A   copy his idea.
   B   use his contacts.
   C   take over his business.

29   Since the company was launched in 2001,

    A   turnover has reached more than £700,000.

    B   the average retail price per map has reached £24.

    C   a total of 200,000 copies of Rainaway maps have been sold.

30   What is the next challenge for Brett's company?

    A   maintaining the effectiveness of its advertising

    B   developing a new range of publications

    C   expanding the size of its call centre

You now have 10 minutes to transfer your answers to your Answer Sheet.

SPEAKING   14 minutes

SAMPLE SPEAKING TASKS

PART ONE

In this part, the interlocutor asks questions to each of the candidates in turn.
You have to give information about yourself and express personal opinions.

PART TWO

In this part of the test, you are asked to give a short talk on a business topic. You
have to choose one of the topics from the three below and then talk for about one
minute. You have one minute to prepare your ideas.

A: What is important when ... ?

Selecting a retail sales assistant
- Previous experience
- Appearance
-
-

B: What is important when ... ?

Contacting clients by telephone
- Calling at the right time
- Listening carefully
-
-

C: What is important when ... ?

Managing change
- Clear objectives
- Communication
-
-

PART THREE

In this part of the test, you are given a discussion topic. You have 30 seconds to look at the task prompt, an example of which is below, and then about three minutes to discuss the topic with your partner. After that, the examiner will ask you more questions related to the topic.

For **two** candidates

Giving Presentations

The Managing Director of the company you work for is concerned about the quality of presentations given by staff at internal and external meetings.

You have been asked to help organise some training for staff in giving presentations.

Discuss the situation together and decide:

- which types of staff would benefit most from this training
- how to decide whether training has been successful.

For **three** candidates

Giving Presentations

The Managing Director of the company you work for is concerned about the quality of presentations given by staff at internal and external meetings.

You have been asked to help organise some training for staff in giving presentations.

Discuss the situation together and decide:

- which types of staff would benefit most from this training
- who would give this training
- how to decide whether training has been successful.

Follow-on questions

- How useful do you think it is for staff to be trained in giving presentations? (Why?/Why not?)

- What do you think makes a successful presentation?

- Would you like to have some training in giving presentations?

- Do you think it's useful to watch other people giving presentations? (Why?/Why not?)

- Do you think it's useful for people to watch video recordings of their own presentations? (Why?/Why not?)

- What other ways of communicating new information to customers and staff might be effective?

Test 4

READING   1 hour

PART ONE

Questions 1–7

- Look at the statements below and the advice on handling acquisitions on the opposite page.
- Which section (**A, B, C** or **D**) does each statement (**1–7**) refer to?
- For each statement (**1–7**), mark one letter (**A, B, C** or **D**) on your Answer Sheet.
- You will need to use some of these letters more than once.

Example:

0 Take the necessary first steps to attract the finance you need for an acquisition.

---

1 A cautious approach can be used when calculating what a company is worth.

2 Consider personnel issues so that you have sufficient resources to fulfill your objectives.

3 In order to know if you can make a return on your investment, assess how you can add to the company you are buying.

4 Providing sufficient support for staff during the acquisition process can have a favourable outcome.

5 Take into account your long-term requirements to ensure you have the resources you need.

6 Even after investing some effort in the acquisition, it may still be necessary to withdraw.

7 Terms initially negotiated can be changed after the acquisition.

Mergers and Acquisitions

As Finance Director of plastics manufacturer VKT, Yvonne Maynart has overseen many successful takeovers

A It is essential to build up a team to handle the acquisition so that your existing business can continue uninterrupted during the deal. It also helps to operate with spare capacity so that you can transfer people during the initial stages. A key person should be driving the acquisition process forward, although one person alone cannot assume responsibility for a large deal. It is clearly vital to do thorough research when identifying potential targets – but do not be afraid to walk away from a deal if you become aware of serious difficulties with a company you are targeting.

B To decide on the value of any target business, you must first determine what contribution your acquisition can make to it. For example, you may be able to increase revenue through a more focused management team, or improve margins through greater purchasing power and lower costs. At VKT, we base our valuations on conservative assumptions – we also add in the risk element. This approach may be best, and it's worth remembering that with listed companies, shareholders tend to have higher risk/reward expectations.

C Developing relationships with finance providers is a key part of the finance director's role. It is important to draw up a good business plan to ensure backing from lenders in the early stages of the acquisition. Your loan application needs to be supported by detailed profit and cashflow projections. Make sure you factor in sufficient finance to let the business develop over time, and allow for reinvestment. Here at VKT, we usually finance acquisitions with bank debt in the form of a 364-day loan, which can then be refinanced at a lower interest rate later.

D If an acquisition is large, it can take years for companies to integrate. At VKT, we monitor all acquisitions closely for at least two years, and the most important lesson I've learned is that a deal is only good if it is beneficial for both vendor and acquirer. Change causes confusion, so it needs to be handled carefully. In order to protect profits and grow the business, you need to minimise the impact of change and help the people affected feel comfortable about it. When this is done properly, it can really boost morale.

PART TWO

Questions 8–12

- Read the article below about marketing partnerships.
- Choose the best sentence from the opposite page to fill each of the gaps.
- For each gap (**8–12**), mark one letter (**A–G**) on your Answer Sheet.
- Do not use any letter more than once.
- There is an example at the beginning (**0**).

When two brands are better than one

Elena Alvarez takes a look at the effectiveness of marketing partnerships

In the corporate world, rivalry is more common than co-operation. But increasingly, companies have been setting aside their differences; the new idea is that two brand names are better than one. Sharing databases, strategies and communication systems can be the most effective means of attracting customers. (**0**) .....G..... This partnership will give it access to the utility company's database of thousands of corporate clients, who will be offered special deals on all its products.

The philosophy behind such joint ventures is simple. In economically challenging times, marketing partnerships provide a cost-effective method of increasing brand awareness and sales. As one expert in the field puts it, 'Clever marketing partnerships allow brands to target the right people, cutting down the above-the-line spend.' (**8**) .... It is better to simplify the process and give them one focal point.

Recent research has indicated that marketing partnerships can be up to 27 per cent more productive than single company campaigns. (**9**) .... In particular, it is ideal for bringing instant branding to companies that lack immediate consumer appeal.

One well-established UK phone manufacturer, ITB, was quick to realise this, and formed an alliance with *Talk*, a leading women's magazine. The phone company has benefited from the strong branding of the magazine, which has its customer base among professional women in their early 20s. (**10**) .... This combined approach also offered ITB a quick route into image enhancement, and this is true of many other marketing partnership deals. To give another illustration, it is no coincidence that some well-known cartoon characters are currently enhancing the image of Nasco household cleaning products. (**11**) .... And, of course, this strategy should also guarantee that consumers' children insist on these products rather than rival brands.

However, while association with a powerful brand can give a significant boost to sales, being connected to a devalued brand can have a negative result. The problems of one brand inevitably impact on the other in a partnership. (**12**) .... A company may take years to recover from this sort of bad publicity. Indeed, there are numerous examples of disastrous marketing alliances. In such cases, not enough thought has been given to the partnership and the reasons behind it, and it has brought little value to either the customer or the companies involved.

Example:

A   In such circumstances, the effects are frequently major and can be long-lasting.

B   Some experts therefore predict that this style of marketing will take up an increasingly large proportion of many companies' total marketing budgets.

C   Successful marketing partnerships can consequently bring a financial advantage even to small and struggling companies such as these.

D   In return, its partner enjoys a broader distribution platform from which to promote its brand.

E   With only a finite number of consumers in any target market, there is no need to overwhelm prospects with competing messages from different organisations.

F   These are fairly standard items, but clearly the company hopes to transform them by broadening the associations consumers have with the brand.

G   For example, Profit Plus, a large UK financial services company, has recently joined forces with a leading supplier of electricity.

PART THREE

Questions 13–18

- Read the article below about the need for language training in the international marketplace and the questions on the opposite page.
- For each question (**13–18**), mark one letter (**A**, **B**, **C** or **D**) on your Answer Sheet.

Speaking Your Customers' Language

Modern international trading practices are highlighting the growing importance of language training

Modern-day business really does transcend national barriers. Thanks to sophisticated IT and communications systems, businesses can now market their products on a truly global scale. The world is indisputably becoming a smaller place, as service and manufacturing companies search the international marketplace for new suppliers and clients. Businesses must, however, be aware that once they expand the area in which they operate, they face increased competition. The standard and quality of their goods become increasingly important in keeping up with competitors. But most of all, it is the service element accompanying the goods which is crucial to a company's success in a particular market. This new philosophy has led to many companies, some of which have even offered products of a lesser quality, gaining success overseas.

Although globalisation may, in some senses, have brought national economies closer together, societies around the world still have radically different expectations, processes and standards. These are not a function of economic change, but are more deep-rooted and difficult to alter. They can be a major problem for businesses expanding abroad, with the greatest obstacle of all being the language barrier. If you have to deal with clients, suppliers and distributors in a range of countries, you will not only need the skills to communicate with them, you will also need to reconcile any national biases you have with the diverse ways of doing business that exist around the globe.

The value of effective communication is not to be underestimated. New technology such as video-conferencing and email has played a part in making the communication process easier, and it may also be possible that the introduction of language interpretation software will help with some global communications problems. But, of course, it is the human element of the communication process that is so vital in business, especially in negotiations, presentations and team-building. It is essential for managers to meet regularly with staff, customers and partners, so that issues can be discussed, messages communicated and feedback obtained.

The value of well-organised language training is immense, and can bring benefits to all levels and departments within a multinational organisation. Unfortunately, however, many organisations have a very narrow view when it comes to training of any kind. Often, an urgent requirement has to be identified before training is authorised. Then, a training company is employed or a programme is developed in-house, the team is trained, and that is seen as the end of the matter. However, the fact remains that training programmes are effective only if they are relevant to a company's broader, long-term needs. They should be regarded as an investment rather than a cost.

Changes in expectations and attitudes are certain to continue for companies that trade globally. Although such companies are not yet faced with their international partners and clients demanding that business be conducted in their mother tongue, they realise that overseas competition is increasing fast. If these companies want to continue to achieve success on the international trading circuit, they must be prepared to adapt to situations and speak the local language. If not, someone else will.

13 According to the first paragraph, improved communications have enabled companies to

    A   offer a wider variety of products and services.

    B   expand beyond their domestic markets.

    C   perform better than their international competitors.

    D   open more manufacturing facilities abroad.

14 Some companies have succeeded at an international level even though they have

    A   produced inferior goods.

    B   failed to adapt products for local markets.

    C   ignored the standards set by their competitors.

    D   reduced the standard of the service they offer.

15 Approaches to doing business vary between countries because of

    A   local economic considerations.

    B   the existence of cultural differences.

    C   strong wishes to remain independent.

    D   regulations about business practices.

16 The writer thinks that the use of modern technology will

    A   speed up the process of language interpretation.

    B   never replace the need for face-to-face interaction.

    C   help solve the problems involved in maintaining strong teams.

    D   not lead to greater communication between companies and clients.

17 A common weakness of training courses is that they

    A   are developed by the wrong team.

    B   do not give good value for money.

    C   are provided only if there is an immediate need.

    D   do not deal with a company's specific requirements.

18 Why should companies do business in the language of the countries they are operating in?

    A   to prevent other companies taking their business

    B   to help them find new international partners

    C   to meet clients' current expectations

    D   to become more aware of their competitors' activities

PART FOUR

Questions 19–33

- Read the article below about a company's results.
- Choose the best word to fill each gap from **A**, **B**, **C** or **D** on the opposite page.
- For each question (**19–33**), mark one letter (**A**, **B**, **C** or **D**) on your Answer Sheet.
- There is an example at the beginning (**0**).

Another successful year

The UK-based agricultural and garden equipment group PLT has had another successful year and is looking forward to the future with (**0**) .....B..... The group, which also has distribution and fuel (**19**) .... , has enjoyed record profits for the fifth year in a (**20**) .... Pre-tax profits for the year (**21**) .... March 31 rose by 24 per cent to £4.2 million.

Total group sales (**22**) .... by five per cent to £155 million, with the agricultural business delivering yet another record (**23**) .... , despite the somewhat difficult trading (**24**) .... in the industry. Sales in the garden equipment (**25**) .... were slow in the early months of the year, but increased dramatically in the final quarter.

Chairman Suresh Kumar said, 'It is my (**26**) .... that we have continued to grow by (**27**) .... our customers well. I am delighted to (**28**) .... the continued development of our customer (**29**) .... and I would like to thank all our customers for their (**30**) .... As well as an increase in customers, our staff numbers also continue to grow. During the year, we have taken (**31**) .... 58 new employees, so that our total workforce now numbers in excess of 700. All of the staff deserve my praise for their dedication and continued efforts in (**32**) .... these excellent results.'

The group has proposed a final (**33**) .... of 9.4p per share, bringing the total to 13p for the year.

Example:

A promise   B confidence   C trust   D security

0	A	B	C	D
	☐	■	☐	☐

19	**A** commitments	**B** interests	**C** responsibilities	**D** benefits
20	**A** row	**B** series	**C** line	**D** sequence
21	**A** completing	**B** closing	**C** finalising	**D** ending
22	**A** extended	**B** lifted	**C** expanded	**D** climbed
23	**A** display	**B** production	**C** performance	**D** demonstration
24	**A** conditions	**B** features	**C** states	**D** aspects
25	**A** part	**B** division	**C** component	**D** side
26	**A** certainty	**B** thought	**C** belief	**D** idea
27	**A** caring	**B** dealing	**C** providing	**D** treating
28	**A** inform	**B** notify	**C** comment	**D** report
29	**A** source	**B** base	**C** foundation	**D** origin
30	**A** support	**B** favour	**C** assistance	**D** service
31	**A** up	**B** back	**C** on	**D** over
32	**A** winning	**B** gaining	**C** achieving	**D** earning
33	**A** dividend	**B** recompense	**C** return	**D** interest

PART FIVE

Questions 34–45

- Read the text below about the use of paper in offices.
- In most of the lines (**34–45**), there is one extra word. It either is grammatically incorrect or does not fit in with the meaning of the text. Some lines, however, are correct.
- If a line is correct, write **CORRECT** on your Answer Sheet.
- If there is an extra word in the line, write **the extra word** in CAPITAL LETTERS on your Answer Sheet.
- The exercise begins with two examples (**0** and **00**).

Examples:	**0**	C	O	R	R	E	C	T		
	00	B	E	E	N					

The Myth of the Paperless Office

0 The concept of a paperless office grew with the advance of technology. It was

00 widely been claimed that as email became commonplace, people would stop

34 writing memos, keeping bulky files and bringing piles of paper to the meetings.

35 But the reality has in fact been quite the reverse, and paper, having already

36 survived five thousand years of technological change, and has proved remarkably

37 resilient. Worldwide, the amount of paper used for each year continues to

38 rise up, although statistics now show a slight reduction in the amount

39 it consumed in the UK. So, has technology failed in its aim to end the use of

40 paper? Max Bray, a business lecturer, thinks office workers still distrust computers.

41 'Technology is unreliable in most of people's eyes,' he says. 'If you are sent an

42 important email, you are likely to print it, because there is always the

43 fear that it might have get deleted.' In contrast, Paul Blunt, a marketing

44 manager for desktop products, who says there has been significant progress in

45 automating a wide range of tasks, even though the transition between has been

more of an evolution than a revolution.

WRITING   45 minutes

PART ONE

- You recently attended an exhibition and saw some equipment you think your company should buy.
- Write an **email** to your company's Purchasing Manager:
  - saying what the equipment is
  - suggesting how the equipment could benefit the company
  - explaining why it is important to place an order soon.
- Write **40–50** words.

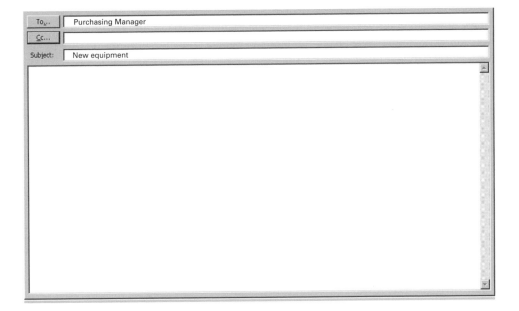

PART TWO

- The company you work for is having problems with Sorenson, one of its suppliers. Your line manager has asked you to write a report giving details and recommending a solution.
- Look at the information below, on which you have already made some handwritten notes.
- Then, using **all** your handwritten notes, write your **report**.
- Write **120–140** words.

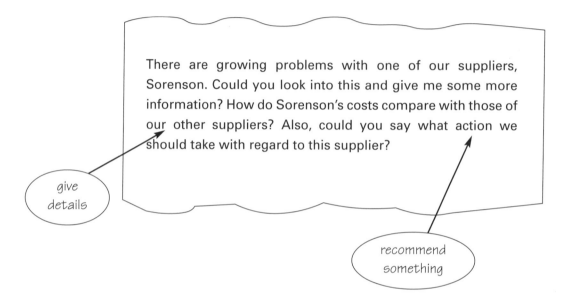

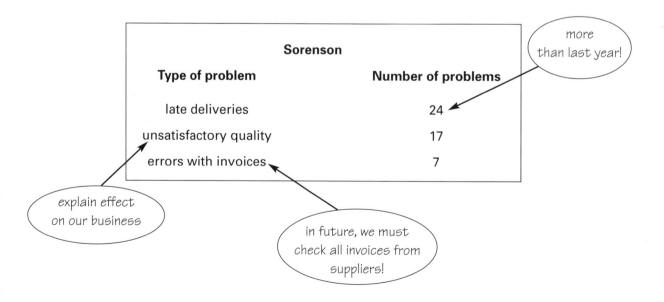

LISTENING   40 minutes (including 10 minutes' transfer time)

PART ONE

Questions 1–12

- You will hear three telephone conversations or messages.
- Write **one** or **two** words or a number in the numbered spaces on the notes or forms below.
- After you have listened once, replay each recording.

Conversation One

(Questions 1–4)

- Look at the note below.
- You will hear a woman telephoning about a seminar.

Telephone Message

For: Amy Johnson

From: Sue Bentley

Re: Seminar 22nd May

New seminar title: (1) ....

Location: (2) ....

Please make copies of the (3) ....

Return her book, (4) '...'

Conversation Two

(Questions 5–8)

- Look at the note below.
- You will hear a man phoning about a delivery.

Message

To: Sarah Williams

From: Brian James

Re: Problem with delivery

We sent him (5) .... paper by mistake.

Call him back straight after your

(6) ....

Please send the right goods or he's threatened to

(7) ....

Also, there's a problem with the payment. He wants to pay by (8) ....

Conversation Three

(Questions 9–12)

- Look at the notes below.
- You will hear a journalist asking for information about a conference.

Day Conference in Newcastle

Run by New Vision Consulting

Date: 10 Oct

Title: (9) ....

Subject: (10) ....

Main Speaker: Daniel Christie, specialist in

(11) ....

Conference will include workshops on

(12) ....

PART TWO

Questions 13–22

Section One

(Questions 13–17)

- You will hear five short recordings.
- For each recording, decide what way of improving profitability the speaker is recommending.
- Write one letter (**A–H**) next to the number of the recording.
- Do not use any letter more than once.
- After you have listened once, replay the recording.

13 ....

14 ....

15 ....

16 ....

17 ....

A	reduce the product range
B	change the policy on prices
C	automate production processes
D	refurbish premises
E	reduce the number of sites
F	increase output
G	reduce staff numbers
H	streamline stock control

Section Two

(Questions 18–22)

- You will hear another five recordings.
- For each recording, decide what the speaker is trying to do.
- Write one letter (**A–H**) next to the number of the recording.
- Do not use any letter more than once.
- After you have listened once, replay the recording.

18 ....

19 ....

20 ....

21 ....

22 ....

A	finalise salaries
B	present forecasts
C	confirm a budget
D	accept a delay
E	postpone investment
F	reject some figures
G	refuse a deadline extension
H	outline a sales strategy

PART THREE

Questions 23–30

- You will hear part of a tutorial between a business student called Gareth and his tutor, in which they discuss Trident Appliances, a manufacturer of photocopiers.
- For each question (**23–30**), mark one letter (**A**, **B** or **C**) for the correct answer.
- After you have listened once, replay the recording.

23 Gareth says that Trident's problem with selling the product is caused by the

    A product specifications.
    B prices that they charge.
    C engineering support.

24 Gareth thinks that the parent company

    A is interested in selling Trident.
    B would like Trident to supply new markets.
    C wants Trident to succeed without any help.

25 In Gareth's opinion, what is the main reason for the workforce being demotivated?

    A changes in pay and conditions
    B lack of job security
    C poor management

26 Gareth thinks that the difficulty for the sales force is caused by

    A having to deal with too many customers.
    B a lack of adequate training.
    C uncertainty about their responsibilities.

27 Gareth says that the service engineers should

    A have a wider role.
    B respond to call-outs more quickly.
    C co-operate more with the Parts Services Department.

28 Gareth suggests that the poor internal communications reflect the middle managers' attitude towards

    A company policies.
    B the employees.
    C senior managers.

29 Gareth thinks that the Chief Executive's most urgent problem is the

    A   product range.
    B   company's turnover.
    C   size of the workforce.

30 Gareth says that the fault in Trident's advertising lies in the

    A   design of the advertisements.
    B   media which are used.
    C   targeting of customers.

You now have 10 minutes to transfer your answers to your Answer Sheet.

SPEAKING   14 minutes

SAMPLE SPEAKING TASKS

PART ONE

In this part, the interlocutor asks questions to each of the candidates in turn.
You have to give information about yourself and express personal opinions.

PART TWO

In this part of the test, you are asked to give a short talk on a business topic. You
have to choose one of the topics from the three below and then talk for about one
minute. You have one minute to prepare your ideas.

A: **What is important when ... ?**

Considering setting up a staff canteen
- Employees' opinions
- Cost to the company
-
-

B: **What is important when ... ?**

Working as a teacher
- Sharing expertise
- Deciding responsibilities
-
-

C: **What is important when ... ?**

Negotiating a contract with a customer
- Customer needs
- Available budget
-
-

PART THREE

In this part of the test, you are given a discussion topic. You have 30 seconds to look at the task prompt card, an example of which is below, and then about three minutes to discuss the topic with your partner. After that, the examiner will ask you more questions related to the topic.

For **two** candidates

Trade Delegation

The company you work for is considering whether to send a trade delegation to a country which is a potential new market.

You have been asked to help plan the trip.

Discuss the situation together and decide:

- what the advantages and disadvantages of sending staff on the trip might be

- what kinds of information about doing business in the country the staff need to know before the trip.

For **three** candidates

Trade Delegation

The company you work for is considering whether to send a trade delegation to a country which is a potential new market.

You have been asked to help plan the trip.

Discuss the situation together and decide:

- what the advantages and disadvantages of sending staff on the trip might be

- what kinds of information about doing business in the country the staff need to know before the trip

- what the company should achieve during the trip.

Follow-on questions

- What other plans for the trip would it be necessary to make in advance?

- What follow-up steps do you think companies should take on returning from a trade delegation?

- If you were offered a place on a trade delegation, would you accept it? (Why?/Why not?)

- What do you think is the best way to give a good impression of a company when doing business abroad? (Why?)

- Why do you think companies sometimes use sales agents to sell their products in other countries?

- How important would it be to speak the language of the country that a trade delegation is visiting? (Why?/Why not?)

KEY

Test 1 Reading

Part 1

1 C   2 D   3 B   4 D   5 A   6 B   7 C

Part 2

8 F   9 C   10 E   11 A   12 D

Part 3

13 B   14 C   15 D   16 B   17 A   18 C

Part 4

19 D   20 B   21 C   22 C   23 A
24 B   25 D   26 C   27 A   28 B
29 B   30 C   31 D   32 B   33 C

Part 5

34 HAVE   35 WHICH   36 FROM
37 UNLESS   38 IS   39 CORRECT
40 CORRECT   41 IN   42 ONLY
43 BOTH   44 CORRECT   45 AS

Test 1 Writing

Part 1

Sample A

> All staff
>
> Budget cuts – meeting
>
> I notice that we are having the meeting next Tuesday. Unfortunally, our buiness has been slow so that why we have made it.
>
> However, please attend all staff, I would like to discuss all staff and tell you about important things.
>
> manager

Band 2

Apart from the fact that one of the content points has not been addressed, the answer contains frequent errors which are distracting, and which have a negative impact on the reader.

Sample B

> Dear colleagues
>
> We are going to have a meeting about the possible cuts in our department's budget on 20th December. This cut is needed because of the loss we made in 2006.
>
> Please attend the meeting because we decide who can take external courses.
>
> Kind regards

Band 4

The answer contains all the necessary information, yet is concise, and the language used is generally accurate. Overall, the impression on the reader is positive.

Part 2

Sample C

> Dear Mr Taylor,
>
> I'm writing to talk about my scheme of installing TV system project. As we know our company is a retail company, so how to attract more customs and how to satisfy the customs is something we should pay attension to. TV system can provide costoms not only the products information in our store but also the services. There's no doubt that TV system can provide convenience and fun to all the people when they shop.
>
> At the same time, the TV system is also available for multi-screens. Normarly, it can get about 20 TV screens needed. So you can get anything you want from the TV.
>
> I know that the system provider also provide training service. They will train our employees to keep them in good scene of using the TV system in a timely manner.
>
> The important thing we might not forget is that the installing of the TV system should be ready in one month. As we cannot impact our operating, and we cannot close our store for long time. They may work overtime to install our TV system and keep it work properly.
>
> That's all my thinking. I'm looking forward to your replying.
> Best wishes!
> yours sincerely
> Holly White
> Dec. 2, 2008

Band 1

Due to misinterpretation of the task, the answer contains irrelevant information and the reader is not adequately informed. Whilst generally being organised satisfactorily, with an adequate range of grammar and vocabulary, there are several errors.

Sample D

> Dear Mr Taylor
>
> I am writing to enquire about your in-store television system we saw advertised in the latest edition of The Daily Mirror. We are a country-wide operating chain of sport shoe shops and are considering to provide our sales rooms with flat screens to entertain our customers and to inform them about our latest inventions.
>
> Due to the fact that we are going to launch a special football shoe next month, we would be pleased if it might be possible for you to install about 20 screens within one month. In addition, we would like to ask further information about your training lessons and we would be grateful if you could send us your detailed brochure as well as your price list.
>
> I look forward to hearing from you and I would appreciate it to receive your information in due course.
>
> Yours sincerely
>
> Christian Van de Watering

Band 5

The candidate's answer is effectively organised, covers all the important information clearly and contains a wide range of vocabulary and structures. There are few errors, and language is well controlled and natural sounding. The overall effect on the reader is very positive.

Test 1   Listening

Part 1

1 PACKAGING
2 PENALTY CLAUSE
3 INSTALLATION
4 INSURANCE
5 (NEW) OUTLETS
6 BRAND EXECUTIVE
7 PURCHASING
8 LOYALTY CARD/SCHEME
9 UPGRADE
10 OVERHEADS
11 PROPERTY
12 PEAK MONTHS

Part 2

| 13 G | 14 H | 15 F | 16 D | 17 B |
| 18 C | 19 F | 20 D | 21 G | 22 B |

Part 3

| 23 A | 24 C | 25 B | 26 A | 27 C |
| 28 A | 29 B | 30 C | | |

Tapescript

Listening Test 1

This is the Business English Certificate Vantage 4. Listening Test 1.

Part One. Questions 1 to 12.

You will hear three telephone conversations or messages.

Write one or two words or a number in the numbered spaces on the notes or forms below.

After you have listened once, replay each recording.

[pause]

Conversation One. Questions 1 to 4.

Look at the note below.

You will hear a man phoning a customer about an order.

You have 15 seconds to read through the note.

[pause]

Now listen, and fill in the spaces.

[pause]

Man: Hello. Could I speak to Bob Cole in Purchasing, please?
Woman: I'm afraid he's out of the office for the day. Can I take a message?
Man: Yes, please. It's Alex Parker from Pilton Engineering.
Woman: Oh yes. We ordered some packaging machines from you, didn't we?
Man: That's right, but I'm going to have to postpone the delivery date. We're having problems finding the right lifting machinery for them.
Woman: I see.

Man: Now, under the terms of the contract I signed, there is a penalty clause for late delivery. But I'm hoping Bob will waive that, since I also agreed to a very good bulk discount.

Woman: I'll check for you.

Man: Thanks. I've decided that, as we're doing the maintenance, I won't charge for installation.

Woman: OK. I've got that.

Man: Oh, and one more thing – I can't find anything in the contract about who's dealing with insurance while the goods are on the road.

Woman: I'll check that.

[pause]

Now listen to the recording again.

[pause]

Conversation Two. Questions 5 to 8.

Look at the notes below.

You will hear a man leaving a message for a colleague about another company's press conference.

You have 15 seconds to read through the notes.

[pause]

Now listen, and fill in the spaces.

[pause]

Man: Hi, Julie, it's Mike, with the information you asked for. Webster's press conference has just finished, and this is what the new Managing Director said about their plans. They've built up healthy profits, which they'll spend on opening new outlets over the next five years. Next, he admitted that they're concerned about their product image, so they've established the new post of Brand Executive reporting to the Marketing Director. They want someone with fresh ideas, who'll make a big difference. Thirdly, since Webster was taken over by the Chilcott Group, they've made savings by centralising logistics, and they'll now apply that process to purchasing. They've examined the feasibility of centralising property operations, but decided against it, at least in the short term. And finally, they plan to increase spending per customer by starting a loyalty card. Experience in the rest of the Chilcott Group shows that customers who join schemes like this spend a third more than other customers. OK, that's all, Julie. Hope it's clear.

[pause]

Now listen to the recording again.

[pause]

Conversation Three. Questions 9 to 12.

Look at the notes below.

You will hear a man telephoning a colleague about a building he has seen.

You have 15 seconds to read through the notes.

[pause]

Now listen, and fill in the spaces.

[pause]

Man: Oh hello, Jan. It's Mark Hill here, the Accommodation Officer. I've just got back from looking at fifteen Lemmington Road, another possible building for our training courses. This one looks very promising. It's in excellent order, and although we might need to adapt some of the rooms, we wouldn't need to upgrade it, unlike some of the other buildings I've seen. The seminar rooms are spacious and airy, and the accommodation is modern and well laid out. The overheads are cheaper than most of the other buildings I've looked at, probably because it's new and well designed. Also on the plus side – it's slightly out of town, so that means less property tax. The downside of that is that it's further from Head Office than some of the other possibilities. The only real problem I can see is its size. It's not a huge building, and during our peak months, it may not be sufficiently large to accommodate all our trainees.

[pause]

Now listen to the recording again.

[pause]

That is the end of Part One. You now have 20 seconds to check your answers.

[pause]

Part Two. Questions 13 to 22.

Section One. Questions 13 to 17.

You will hear five short recordings. Five speakers are talking about the use of technology in recruitment.

For each recording, decide what recommendation the speaker makes concerning technology in recruitment.

Write one letter (A–H) next to the number of the recording.

Do not use any letter more than once.

After you have listened once, replay the recordings.

You now have 15 seconds to read the list A–H.

[pause]

Now listen, and decide what recommendation each speaker makes concerning technology in recruitment.

[pause]

Thirteen
I'm the company's recruitment specialist, and we've moved heavily into using the internet. It's virtually eliminated the sorts of applications that don't stand a chance. We have an online application system that works well, because it elicits the vital information at the outset. For instance, there might be something like 'Do you have hands-on experience of the latest technologies in this field?' People who can't give the answers are immediately advised not to continue with their application.

[pause]

Fourteen
It's astonishing that, while nearly all British businesses use the internet in one way or another, most of them just use their websites as shop windows for advertising jobs – then expect people to send in paper-based applications. They're simply not using the technology to its best advantage. There are so many refinements that the internet makes possible, so every recruitment officer ought to be looking at making optimal use of it and cutting out as much paper as they can.

[pause]

Fifteen
Many companies think they're up to date if they advertise vacancies on their website and send emails to applicants instead of letters. But that just isn't enough. These days, lots of people send text messages, so businesses should follow suit, for instance when inviting someone to interview: it shows that the firm has joined the twenty-first century. And although the phone is much more traditional, it's still a valuable form, because you can talk to applicants in person.

[pause]

Sixteen
Companies sometimes get the wrong idea about online recruitment. They focus on the fact that it can reduce administration, but forget that it takes specific skills to manage the online process. After all, the recruitment section of the website needs to be organised, applications dealt with quickly and effectively, and so on. People who are used to circulating details of vacancies internally, planning newspaper advertising, acknowledging applications, etc. may not have the abilities required for dealing with online recruitment.

[pause]

Seventeen
So often, people apply for jobs they know very little about, because positions with the same title can vary considerably in different organisations. So when you're recruiting, you should use your website to list projects and assignments of the post and give case histories of people in similar posts in the company, perhaps with a personal statement from them. It doesn't affect the procedure you follow, but it helps potential applicants to decide if it's a job they really want.

[pause]

Now listen to the recordings again.

[pause]

Section Two. Questions 18 to 22.

You will hear another five recordings. Five speakers are talking about how to deal with complaints about goods.

For each recording, decide what action the speaker is recommending.

Write one letter (A–H) next to the number of the recording.

Do not use any letter more than once.

After you have listened once, replay the recordings.

You have 15 seconds to read the list A–H.

[pause]

Now listen, and decide what action each speaker is recommending.

[pause]

Eighteen
Some people tell you that what a dissatisfied customer really wants is to have the opportunity to spend his money again. You may have to resort to

this – a refund or perhaps some form of credit. However, this may lose a customer and will certainly lose that particular deal. Try a bit of persuasion – remind your customer why he chose your product in the first place, give him a new one and save him the trouble of making further decisions.

[pause]

Nineteen

It's often the case that a complaint about faulty equipment really means the customer is doing something wrong. Of course, considerable tact is called for when this happens – don't make them feel foolish. What they need is some guidance – and this should be provided without further cost. Make sure any damage done has been put right, and then set up the familiarisation session. Problem solved, customer happy, equipment saved from any more misuse.

[pause]

Twenty

When a customer complains, it's important to be sympathetic, but business-like as well. Do apologise, of course, and then, taking a personal interest in the way the equipment will be used, suggest a newer, more recent model rather than simply replacing the original one. This is often a good solution, because it not only deals with the complaint, but also the client feels they've got away with a bit extra to make up for the inconvenience.

[pause]

Twenty-one

I don't think all complaints can be dealt with in the same way. Basically, you've got to solve the immediate problem to try to keep the customer's confidence. Sometimes guaranteeing your product for a longer period can be a good way to do this. Fix what's wrong as quickly as possible and show you're prepared to do so a second time if necessary. Point out that the customer won't have any worries, at least not until they need an upgrade.

[pause]

Twenty-two

It's a good idea to let the customer know why there's been a problem – it shows you are prepared to be honest, and you might win a bit of sympathy. They realise that things don't always go right for the supplier either. But the most satisfactory thing to do is to offer a refund. Then, of course, they are more likely to deal with you again when they need a replacement.

[pause]

Now listen to the recordings again.

[pause]

That is the end of Part Two.

[pause]

Part Three. Questions 23 to 30.

You will hear John Sergeant, a retail analyst, being interviewed about a chain of clothing stores called Sangra.

For each question, 23–30, mark one letter (A, B or C) for the correct answer.

After you have listened once, replay the recording.

You have 45 seconds to read through the questions.

[pause]

Now listen, and mark A, B or C.

Woman: The big clothing retailer Sangra is currently in the news, and here to talk about its difficulties is retail analyst John Sergeant.

Man: Hello.

Woman: John, why have Sangra's sales fallen so much?

Man: Well, they've started using top designers, but it takes too long to get the designs from the drawing board into the shops. Sangra haven't realised that fashion trends are moving faster than ever, and they need to react much more quickly. As a result, they aren't attracting younger shoppers. It really makes little difference who designs their clothes or what the stores look like if people don't feel like going in.

Woman: They've been very short-sighted, haven't they?

Man: That's right. Sangra's strength is in the middle market, but shoppers now want either expensive designer labels or low prices. At the same time, other stores have started to compete for the same customers, but are offering lower prices. Sangra's response to these dangers has been an advertising campaign which was right off target, and which actually seems to have lost them customers. And amazingly, they're still running it.

Woman: The last Chief Executive was thought to be responsible for many of the mistakes, wasn't he?

Man: Throughout the nineteen nineties, the company was managed by Denis Howard, who was a strong leader. He decided on the policy of acquisition, and to be fair to him, he managed to persuade the Board. But when sales fell, Howard was forced out. If he'd already got somebody in position to take over, everything might have been fine, but as it was, a boardroom argument broke out. That's when the company's problems started.

Woman: So what's happening now?

Man: The new management's started a high-cost policy of introducing what they call the 'lifestyle' idea into the stores, grouping merchandise according to the target customer. For example, instead of dresses in one area, shoes in another, they have one section aimed at active adults, another at teenagers, and so on. The staff seem to be behind them, but they're finding that most of the stores just don't have the floor space for it.

Woman: Is this the solution to the company's problems?

Man: Not really. They're also trying to make savings, like cutting the number of higher-paid staff to improve productivity; but the effect is minimal. The fact is that margins in retailing are being cut, and Sangra will have to do the same if they're to succeed. I'm sure this will be their next step. Or else they'll have to start shutting poorly performing stores, but that means shutting all of them.

Woman: Do you think it's suffering from its old-fashioned, top-down style of management?

Man: Yes, but they're beginning to change. They're going to have to take much more notice of what shoppers want, but at the moment, they're working to reduce the time it takes for new products to be manufactured, so for the first time they and their suppliers are co-operating to make improvements. To be honest, if the management were less autocratic, they could also learn a lot from their staff.

Woman: What would be *your* advice to Sangra?

Man: They need to remember that their years of success came from supplying a broad range of ordinary clothes. They've made too many mistakes recently, like moving into designer items. They should stop playing with new ideas and just do what they're good at. There isn't really a safe alternative.

Woman: How is the company likely to change in the next few years?

Man: Their main activity will still be the same, even if they decide to follow the trend into big out-of-town stores. Their venture into financial services and food halls, both of which are due to start this year, will have a considerable effect, though whether for good or bad remains to be seen. And we may well find Sangra stores opening abroad, and my guess is that it'll be through acquisition.

Woman: John Sergeant, thank you very much.

Man: Thank you.

[pause]

Now listen to the recording again.

[pause]

That is the end of Part Three. You now have ten minutes to transfer your answers to your Answer Sheet.

[pause]

Note: Teacher, stop the recording here and time ten minutes. Remind students when there is **one** minute remaining.

That is the end of the test.

Test 2   Reading

Part 1

1 B	2 D	3 A	4 C	5 B	6 C
7 D					

Part 2

8 C	9 F	10 D	11 A	12 E

Part 3

13 B	14 A	15 D	16 D	17 C
18 B				

Part 4

19 B	20 C	21 D	22 B	23 A
24 D	25 A	26 C	27 C	28 A
29 D	30 C	31 B	32 D	33 B

Part 5

34 WHICH
35 CORRECT
36 ON
37 CORRECT
38 BUT
39 UP
40 THOSE
41 ADDITIONALLY
42 BOTH
43 TOO
44 MUCH
45 WHILE

Test 2   Writing

Part 1

Sample A

> Hi,
> As you know this department has increased a lot, because of that, we are going to introduce identity cards. Only the employees that entered in the department until 2008, will need this cards. You can get this cards in the administration department.

Band 3

All content points have been addressed, and the organisation and register of the email are on the whole satisfactory. The range of vocabulary and grammar is adequate, and although there are a number of errors, these are minor and do not prevent the message being clearly conveyed.

Sample B

> Dear colleagues,
>
> I am writing to inform you that everyone being involved in software development will need be provided with an identity card by the service team on next Monday. Due to stolen data the head office decided to prevent unauthorised access to data this way.
>
> Regards,
>
> Alex Thierry

Band 4

All points are addressed, and the register and format are on the whole appropriate. The range and accuracy of language are generally good, and the reader would be clearly and fully informed.

Part 2

Sample C

> For number of Parkside staff leaving stores problem, I made a report as follows:
>
> At first, look at draw, from this one you can see, Year 2007. Highgate lost 4 person. Parkside lost 5. Until 2008, Highgate's rate is reduced, but Parkside's rate is grew so high more staff leaving will make the store pay more time & money employ another one instead of this one. This is waste to the manual resource & money.
>
> Through communicate with the Parkside staff, I know there are three point very important.
>
> Firstly, training wanted. The staff want to more training to improve themselves' level. everyday their make the same job, long and long, their will hate this job. I think the company need to provide this benefit to the staff.
>
> Secondly. More paid holiday. I think this is the first, but the staff is not pay attention it, so that is not possible.
>
> Thirdly. Bonus Scheme. if the company can pay more money employ the new staff why cannot pay more salary to the current staff? So I suggest the company provide the double-salary as the bonus pay for the current staff end of the years.
>
> That's all.
>
> Sincerely,
>
> Lucy.

Band 2

The report is considerably longer than the recommended word length and does not cover all the content points. Although the report is adequately paragraphed, cohesion is weak. The register and format of the report are not always appropriate; errors are numerous and impede clear communication of the message.

Sample D

Report on staff turnover

Introduction

This report aims to explain the high staff turnover 2008 in Parkside and to propose measures to improve staff loyalty.

Findings

The figures clearly show that the high number of staff leaving the stores is a problem that only affects the Parkside store in 2008. While staff turnover in the Highgate store remained on a low level the number of staff leaving Parkside shoot up from 5 to 20. This unfortunately has a bad impact on customer service.

Research amongst staff revealed their requirements. Firstly staff requires more training what would also benefit the company as the service is likely to improve. Another good idea is the introduction of a bonus scheme for valued staff that would improve staff loyalty. Unlike the mentioned proposals the request for a longer annual lave could not be met.

Recommendations

It is recommended to offer both the requested training opportunities and a bonus scheme for valued staff.

Band 5

All content points are clearly covered, and the report is well organised with good cohesion. Both the register and format are consistently appropriate. Generally, the language used is accurate, and a good range of structures and vocabulary is demonstrated.

Test 2   Listening

Part 1

1 (THE) LAST QUARTER
2 (THE) LONG(-)TERM
3 CURRENT
4 LOSSES
5 SECOND STAGE
6 (A) PENALTY (CLAUSE)
7 UNSKILLED
8 (ANOTHER)/(A)/(THE) CONTRACT
9 (SOFTWARE) ENGINEER
10 (THE) TIMING
11 (THE) HARDWARE
12 OBJECTIVE(S)

Part 2

13 C	14 B	15 F	16 H	17 D
18 F	19 D	20 G	21 H	22 C

Part 3

23 C	24 B	25 A	26 A	27 C
28 A	29 B	30 B		

Tapescript

Listening Test 2

This is the Business English Certificate Vantage 4, Listening Test 2.

Part One. Questions 1 to 12.

You will hear three telephone conversations or messages.

Write one or two words or a number in the numbered spaces on the notes or forms below.

After you have listened once, replay each recording.

[pause]

Conversation One. Questions 1 to 4.

Look at the note below.

You will hear a man clarifying some information about a balance sheet.

You have 15 seconds to read through the note.

[pause]

Now listen, and fill in the spaces.

[pause]

Man: Hi, Tom here. Could I speak with Bill?

Key

Woman: Sorry, he's out. Can I take a message?

Man: Thanks. It's about some queries Bill had about the balance sheet I prepared.

Woman: Which balance sheet exactly? The one for the last financial year?

Man: Actually, it was the one for the last quarter.

Woman: OK, got that.

Man: There were several things Bill wanted to check. Firstly, he asked about the liabilities figures. He thought the figures in column A might be for current liabilities, but in fact those figures indicate the long-term ones.

Woman: OK, I've got that. What next?

Man: The assets figures. He wondered exactly what they cover. Actually, I've put the current assets there, but I've still got to work out the fixed assets and the intangible assets before I include them.

Woman: Thanks. Anything else?

Man: One last thing. Also about assets. Bill wasn't sure what the figures in brackets in section four refer to. He thought they might represent average figures for the last two years or something like that. In fact, they show losses over that period.

Woman: Thanks. I'll pass all that on.

[pause]

Now listen to the recording again.

[pause]

Conversation Two. Questions 5 to 8.

Look at the notes below.

You will hear a man leaving a voicemail message about a negotiating problem.

You have 15 seconds to read through the notes.

[pause]

Now listen, and fill in the spaces.

[pause]

Hi, George. This is Kristoff calling from Australia. It's about the contract negotiation for constructing the factory in Melbourne. Our client doesn't want to agree the date for the completion of the second stage, even though it was accepted when we put in our tender. We specified that we couldn't complete in less than six months. Now they're saying they want it brought forward a month. This is a problem, because they want to put in a penalty clause which states that for every week we are late, we have to pay three per cent of the total cost. I can't agree to this at all. We're already using our best technical employees, and the only way we can

complete in five months is if we use more unskilled staff right from the beginning, which'll mean a substantial investment which we hadn't budgeted for. There's one incentive, however; instead of the usual bonus, we'll be awarded the contract for their next project if we can meet their new deadline.

[pause]

Now listen to the recording again.

[pause]

Conversation Three. Questions 9 to 12.

Look at the notes below.

You will hear a woman telephoning a colleague about a new project.

You have 15 seconds to read through the notes.

[pause]

Now listen, and fill in the spaces.

[pause]

Man: Hello. Joe Fischer speaking.

Woman: Joe, it's Wilma here. Can I have a word with you about the e-commerce website?

Man: Of course. How did the interviews go?

Woman: Well, we recruited an excellent business analyst this morning – he'll join the team in a week or so. There's still a gap for a software engineer, though, and we'll have to fill that as soon as possible.

Man: I'll ask around and see if anyone is able to transfer from other projects.

Woman: Thanks. Also, do you think you could produce a report for senior management by the end of the week? They'd like an idea of the timing of the project.

Man: No problem. What else should I include?

Woman: Let us know exactly what hardware you'll need. The budget already allows for that.

Man: OK – anything else?

Woman: Yes – when you describe the project, would you make sure you spell out the objectives in clear, straightforward language? Certain members of the Board have their doubts that it will bring about the results we promised.

Man: OK.

[pause]

Now listen to the recording again.

[pause]

That is the end of Part One. You now have 20 seconds to check your answers.

[pause]

Part Two. Questions 13 to 22.

Section One. Questions 13 to 17.

You will hear five short recordings.

For each recording, decide which aspect of conducting interviews each speaker considers particularly important.

Write one letter (A–H) next to the number of the recording.

Do not use any letter more than once.

After you have listened once, replay the recordings.

You have 15 seconds to read the list A–H.

[pause]

Now listen, and decide which aspect each speaker considers important.

[pause]

Thirteen
We all forget how hard interviews can be. Applicants walk into a strange room and face what can be a long line of unknown people who fire a lot of tricky questions at them. It's not surprising that their minds go a complete blank. If you're the interviewer and you make an effort to put the interviewees at their ease, then they're more likely to express their opinions coherently and give you a chance to assess them properly.

[pause]

Fourteen
Interviews are often too theoretical. You get the applicant's views on, for example, the principles of marketing and then throw in some tough questions to see if they're up to speed on the latest developments. But introducing a hands-on activity can be more telling, because then you can assess how they approach everyday activities. I know some people argue that at senior level it's a waste of time and you should be checking how they deal with clients and colleagues, but I'm not convinced.

[pause]

Fifteen
You have perhaps thirty minutes to assess an applicant. I think considerable work needs to be done beforehand with the CVs – checking if they have appropriate qualifications and so on. What you can't get from the application, though – except from references, and I don't find those very reliable – is an idea of how people act in the workplace. I focus on that, by asking questions which should reveal how they'd react in different circumstances and with a variety of colleagues.

[pause]

Sixteen
Interviewing isn't something I'm good at, I'm afraid. I don't trust my own judgement for such important decisions. That's why I usually have about five other people with me, not necessarily from the particular department, though. I realise this prevents me from making the interview seem like an informal chat, but I'm not sure of the overall benefit of that – perhaps it provides an insight into how the applicant thinks and behaves outside work, but that's not crucial.

[pause]

Seventeen
One's trying to assess so many different aspects of potential employees. Time's limited, and you can get bogged down in asking challenging questions relevant to particular duties in the job description. It's easy to forget to allow time for applicants to find out things that are relevant to them. It's sometimes seen just as a courtesy or a way of making them feel comfortable, but it can give you real insight into how they think and react to the post.

[pause]

Now listen to the recordings again.

[pause]

Section Two. Questions 18 to 22.

You will hear another five recordings. Five speakers are talking about problems with a project.

For each recording, decide what the problem was.

Write one letter (A–H) next to the number of the recording.

Do not use any letter more than once.

After you have listened once, replay the recordings.

You have 15 seconds to read the list A–H.

[pause]

Now listen, and decide what each problem was.

[pause]

Eighteen
Well, we'd put together what we thought was an excellent team for the project – that is, until we hit technical problems and realised that we needed

107

staff with a wider range of specialised technical experience than the people we'd recruited. So we had to advertise again to replace some key members of the team; we were lucky that we just about managed to cover the extra costs within the budget. Our customers were very satisfied with the outcome.

[pause]

Nineteen
Although we had minor problems with suppliers from the start, these were easily overcome. Initially, I thought we'd underestimated the cost of the project, as it was so tight most of the time, but we managed to avoid an overspend. It was a very stressful time. However, it was the breakdowns which really upset the staff, and I wouldn't have blamed them if they'd walked out on strike the fifth time it happened in a week.

[pause]

Twenty
Generally speaking, we have an excellent project-management team, trained to deal with any unexpected problems – you know, like when the money runs out or the client wants something different from the original agreement. Unfortunately, we hadn't anticipated the component manufacturer going out of business. The Purchasing Manager was furious, because there were so few companies who produced exactly what we wanted. However, finally we found a replacement that enabled us to keep within the limits of our budget.

[pause]

Twenty-one
We've done several projects in this country, and the best thing about working here is that suppliers are very helpful. If you are unhappy with anything, they immediately try and sort it out. If, for example, a digger broke down, they'd replace it within hours and at no extra cost. Another thing is there is no shortage of suitably qualified workers, but we had an expensive delay on our last project, because we'd miscalculated the size of the workforce we needed.

[pause]

Twenty-two
We spent so much time making sure that our employees would be comfortable working in such difficult conditions. We warned them about what to expect, as well as checking that they had the

right qualifications and experience. We thought we'd anticipated every possible problem. This time, we were proved wrong when the supplier sent us different trucks from the ones ordered. Although they coped well with the extreme conditions, they were too small for our needs.

[pause]

Now listen to the recordings again.

[pause]

That is the end of Part Two.

[pause]

Part Three. Questions 23–30.

You will hear a radio reporter talking about difficulties faced by the new Chief Executive of Healthway plc, a chain of health and beauty stores.

For each question, 23–30, mark one letter (A, B or C) for the correct answer.

After you have listened once, replay the recording.

You have 45 seconds to read through the questions.

[pause]

Now listen, and mark A, B or C.

[pause]

Man: Next week, Healthway plc, the health and beauty chain, gets a new Chief Executive. Here's our reporter, Lynne Trencher, to tell us why many people regard the job as one of the most difficult in retailing. Hello, Lynne.

Woman: Hello. No, it isn't an enviable position. Robert Henlow, Healthway's new CEO, is taking control of a company which may have been a well-loved and trusted retail brand for many years, but its core business is mature, and successive managements simply haven't come up with a winning formula to deliver dynamic sales growth. And the shareholders see Henlow as Healthway's last chance.

Man: The company faces stiff competition, doesn't it?

Woman: That's right. In fact, most town-centre health and beauty chains are feeling the pinch, with few planning to expand. Unlike food, it's a high-margin business, which gives supermarkets, particularly those on out-of-town sites, scope to sell similar products for considerably less. Even the development of online shopping hasn't yet outweighed the convenience of out-of-town sites.

Man: Robert Henlow is coming from a company with a very different sort of culture from Healthway, isn't he?

Woman: Yes, he's moving from a firm that's very open, with plenty of staff coming in from other companies, or indeed industries. Healthway, on the other hand, has a culture where people join the group and either leave quickly, or not until they retire. It's famous for breeding its own managers, and outsiders have traditionally not been welcomed.

Man: Healthway's financial strategy has been criticised in recent years, I believe.

Woman: Under the last Chief Executive, Charles Hamilton, Healthway concentrated on the bottom line, with the aim of supporting the share price. Even the one acquisition that the company made had that same goal. But this strategy had its downside: very few improvements were made within the business, so their IT, for instance, is now several years out of date.

Man: Wasn't it Charles Hamilton who started Healthway's beauty treatment centres?

Woman: Yes, almost his first major action as Chief Executive was to set up a separate chain of stores that, in addition to selling health and beauty products, provided massage and other treatments. This ran alongside the existing stores. But even at the outset, few investors were taken in by his over-optimistic forecasts, and the doubters were proved right. Just before he left the company, he closed the centres and admitted his mistake.

Man: Hamilton also made drastic staffing changes, didn't he?

Woman: He certainly did: he slimmed down the head office, he undertook a complete overhaul of the top management team and tidied up the company's international operations. Of course, there was a danger that in changes on that scale, mistakes would be made and the company would lose individuals, or even whole departments, that it needed. He managed to avoid that, but he was quite unable to communicate the reasons behind the changes, so he created an enormous amount of ill will.

Man: Hm. Has Robert Henlow announced any plans yet?

Woman: When he starts work next Monday, he'll find a report from consultants, advising the disposal of several underperforming stores that are too small ever to do well. However, they do think the current total should be maintained, which would be achieved by ploughing money into more profitable large-store formats. Even though this means adding to the payroll, the consultants say the increased profitability will make it worthwhile.

Man: So, all in all, it's quite a challenge for Robert Henlow.

Woman: It certainly is, not least because he's never run a quoted company of this size before, and he's one of the youngest chief executives of a business like this. He's taking a huge step from his previous position, though at least the health and beauty sector isn't entirely new to him. He's not going to find it at all easy to tackle all Healthway's problems.

Man: Lynne, thank you.

[pause]

Now listen to the recording again.

[pause]

That is the end of Part Three. You now have ten minutes to transfer your answers to your Answer Sheet.

[pause]

Note: Teacher, stop the recording here and time ten minutes. Remind students when there is **one** minute remaining.

That is the end of the test.

Test 3   Reading

Part 1

1 B	2 A	3 D	4 B	5 C	6 A
7 C					

Part 2

8 E	9 A	10 D	11 B	12 F

Part 3

13 C	14 C	15 A	16 D	17 B
18 D				

Part 4

19 D	20 A	21 A	22 B	23 C
24 B	25 C	26 B	27 C	28 A
29 D	30 C	31 B	32 D	33 C

Part 5

34 YET   35 OF   36 IMPROVE
37 BEEN   38 THIS   39 FROM
40 ALLOW   41 THE   42 THAT
43 CORRECT   44 EXTRA   45 CORRECT

Test 3   Writing

Part 1

Sample A

> Dear All
>
> I am writing to inform you that I am going to change a department next Monday 5 May.
>
> In My new position will take place in the Marketing department, where I am going to be responsible of promoting the new products. And also to ensure their productivity.
>
> Regards

Band 3

The candidate has addressed all the content points. The answer is concise, and although it contains a number of errors, these do not impede communication. The overall effect on the reader is satisfactory.

Sample B

> To: all staff
> From: Karen Müller / Sales Manager
> Date: June 2nd , 2007
> Subject: Department Transfer
>
> Dear Colleagues,
>
> I would like you to know that I will leave this department in order to take over a new job in the purchasing department.
>
> My new employment will start on July 1st , 2007 and my main duty will be to negotiate supply contracts.
>
> Thank you.
> Karen

Band 5

The candidate has fully addressed all the content points. The language is natural and well controlled in its usage. The overall effect on the reader is very positive.

Part 2

Sample C

> I considered all the effects in our Company, and found not closing village store is a well choice at this moment. Since it is far from the city, the people in the village have poor ability to buy our product, and customers become more and more less. If we could reduce the price, we may get a good benefit and for a another important reason, village store have not reached a high level and full equipment.
>
> Due to the town have developed for the nearest four years, more and more people wanted to try enjoy our service. and the profits are better than before. I think we could spend more time and money to expend it to get more profits.
>
> Ou-of-town market have a great changes during these years. Many people like to visit these place when the free time. meantime, nesseary equipment is important to them. people like our service and want more.
>
> Regarding the three kinds of store, we should closed the village store, and develop the other two stores. We could open more markting on these 2 kinds of store to get more profit.
>
> Hope this is clear and thank you very much.
>
> B rgds
> Kim Jung

Band 2

The candidate has attempted to address all the content points using an appropriate register and format. However, due to poor language control and numerous errors, the message is not clearly conveyed. The overall effect on the reader is negative.

Sample D

> We have the following facts to consider:
> – village store
>   with £20,000 very low profit
>   Decision: there are to many shops within this area, which provide the same choice of products.
>
> – town-centre store
>   quite profitable with £130,000, we didn't expect such good figures. This shop is well placed in a busy shopping zone with also a lot of tourists.
>
> – out-of-town superstore
>   very successful with an excellent profit of £250,000. This shop profits from enough parking places in front of the store and different shops and outlets arround.
>
> If we have to close a store in our region, I would propose to give up the village store. Regarding new service in the other shops I would imagine that an internet access would be interesting for our customers. This service doesn't exist around and could shorten waiting times for escating people.

Band 4
The candidate has addressed all the content points, using a good range of appropriate vocabulary and structures. The report is well organised and generally accurate. The overall effect on the reader is positive.

Test 3   Listening

Part 1

1 JOBSPLAN
2 CURRENT REPORTS
3 (THE) APPENDIX
4 (THE) HEAD OFFICE
5 (THE) DISCOUNT SHOP
6 DELIVERIES
7 SURVEY
8 TAX BENEFITS
9 SHAREHOLDERS(')
10 VIP LOUNGE
11 SOUND SYSTEM
12 EVENTS

Part 2

| 13 D | 14 A | 15 F | 16 C | 17 H |
| 18 E | 19 H | 20 D | 21 C | 22 G |

Part 3

| 23 C | 24 A | 25 B | 26 C | 27 B |
| 28 C | 29 A | 30 A | | |

Tapescript

Listening Test 3

This is the Business English Certificate Vantage 4, Listening Test 3.

Part One. Questions 1 to 12.

You will hear three telephone conversations or messages.

Write one or two words or a number in the numbered spaces on the notes or forms below.

After you have listened once, replay each recording.

[pause]

Conversation One. Questions 1 to 4.

Look at the notes below.

You will hear a phone conversation between a manager and his PA.

You have 15 seconds to read through the notes.

[pause]

Now listen, and fill in the spaces.

[pause]

Man: Hi, Jane. Barry here. Sorry this is a bit rushed, but I need you to fax me a document urgently.
Woman: No problem. What do you need?
Man: That report I've been writing on recruitment. I haven't printed it off, but you'll find it on my computer. I called it 'jobsplan', all one word. OK?
Woman: No problem. Which folder is it in? Personnel?
Man: That's right. No, no, hang on, um, I created a new folder called Current Reports – it's in there.
Woman: OK. I've made a note of that. If I can't locate it, I'll call you back.

Man: Fine. It's quite a long document by the way. So don't bother sending the appendix. We don't really need that. But include the contents page – that'd be quite useful.

Woman: Shall I send it to you there at Head Office?

Man: Um . . . let me think. It might be better to fax it to my hotel. Er, no, you're right. Send it here.

Woman: OK.

Man: Thanks very much. Bye.

[pause]

Now listen to the recording again.

[pause]

Conversation Two. Questions 5 to 8.

Look at the notes below.

You will hear two colleagues discussing an additional location for their business.

You have 15 seconds to read through the notes.

[pause]

Now listen, and fill in the spaces.

[pause]

Woman: Hello, Mike, have you got a moment?

Man: Sure, what is it? The location?

Woman: Yes, we can't put it off any longer.

Man: Hm, especially as we chose the site for the new warehouse last night. We need to get organised.

Woman: Exactly. We need a decision today. Where should the discount shop be, then?

Man: Well, not too close to our existing branches, that's for sure. I think it'd better be in the out-of-town retail centre.

Woman: I know that's easier for customers, but the business park, which is the *other* out-of-town site, would be better for deliveries, which is important.

Man: But the trend is towards more and more people using the retail centre, isn't it?

Woman: Well, the survey we did shows people *will* visit the business park if we open there.

Man: Really? I wasn't expecting that. Is it because we produce specialist goods? Does that make a difference?

Woman: Yes.

Man: Are there any local grants available?

Woman: Not as such, but there are tax benefits if we take on premises in the business park.

Man: Right. That's settled, then. How about . . .

[pause]

Now listen to the recording again.

[pause]

Conversation Three. Questions 9 to 12.

Look at the note below.

You will hear a woman leaving a message about where to hold a meeting.

You have 15 seconds to read through the note.

[pause]

Now listen, and fill in the spaces.

[pause]

Hi, it's Emily Parker in Marketing. I was at the Carlton Hotel yesterday for a sales training meeting. I thought it would be a very suitable place to hold the shareholders' meeting you're arranging. I heard you're still looking for somewhere. They've recently refurbished all their meeting rooms. I was in a seminar room – it was too small for your event, but I looked at the conference hall and the VIP lounge and either would be perfect – oh, except the conference hall's booked on the twenty-fifth of October, so it doesn't leave us any choice. Anyway, they're both large rooms with comfortable seating, and it's possible to have a sound system at no extra cost. We'd have to bring a display stand of our own if we wanted one. Assuming you want to go ahead with the twenty-fifth, I mentioned to the Events Manager there that we might want to book, so you'll need to talk to him, rather than the General Manager in the bookings office. The number's three-five-seven-two-oh-nine. Bye.

[pause]

Now listen to the recording again.

[pause]

That is the end of Part One. You now have 20 seconds to check your answers.

[pause]

Part Two. Questions 13 to 22.

Section One. Questions 13 to 17.

You will hear five short recordings. Five speakers are talking about delegating at work.

For each recording, decide what advice the speaker gives about delegating at work.

Write one letter (A–H) next to the number of the recording.

Do not use any letter more than once.

After you have listened once, replay the recordings.

You have 15 seconds to read the list A–H.

[pause]

Now listen, and decide what advice each speaker gives about delegating at work.

[pause]

Thirteen
No matter how much confidence you have in the person you're entrusting a task to, I think there's a crucial element to delegating that's often forgotten. There has to be a framework in place of where and who to go to if they get stuck and need help. I know, as a manager, I'm used to dealing with tasks all by myself, but when I'm delegating to juniors, I always remind myself that not everybody is as independent as me.

[pause]

Fourteen
If you've ever delegated to someone else and spent more time on the task than if you'd done it yourself, then it's time to review where you're going wrong. If your motivation for delegating is thinking that the other person can do it better than you, or it'll free you up to do something else, that's great. But delegation isn't an easy way out, so if you're just being lazy or the task seems too small to concern yourself with, always do it yourself.

[pause]

Fifteen
Once you've selected someone to delegate a task to – assuming you do have a choice of personnel – there's something you need to do that's too important to leave till the job's finished. It's a mistake if you don't make it clear to staff what they're doing well and what they could improve on. Some managers think it's a form of interfering and doesn't give people space to get on with the job, but I find some constructive suggestions are usually helpful.

[pause]

Sixteen
When you give someone a task to do, there's not much point in simply listing the particular difficulties involved in carrying it out. You really need to check they understand what challenges they can expect to face and how they might deal with them. So you should sit down with them and explore possible solutions. If they simply say 'I understand', it's not a guarantee that they do.

[pause]

Seventeen
Once you become an effective delegator, you'll be talked about by those who see what you and your team can achieve. And, as for team members, well, they'll appreciate the trust you place in them and the support they've received from you. But until you reach that point on the learning curve, keep telling yourself not to give up whenever it doesn't go to plan. I've certainly had some disastrous attempts at delegating in my time.

[pause]

Now listen to the recordings again.

[pause]

Section Two. Questions 18 to 22.

You will hear another five recordings. Five speakers are talking about the reason for the success of their company's most recent TV advertising campaign.

For each recording, decide what reason the speaker gives for the success of the campaign.

Write one letter (A–H) next to the number of the recording.

Do not use any letter more than once.

After you have listened once, replay the recordings.

You have 15 seconds to read the list A–H.

[pause]

Now listen, and decide what each speaker says is the reason for the success.

[pause]

Eighteen
Our last campaign was the most successful ever. Always worried about the cost, we were on a tight budget, but the results were fantastic. Research had shown our rivals' products were more attractive, but while the ad was running, one of them had some bad publicity about their products, and we picked up a lot of their trade. Sometimes, it's not how much you invest or who you use, but just being in the right place at the right time.

[pause]

Nineteen
Last year's TV campaign took the market by storm. In the past, we'd depended heavily on sending out samples to customers – it was a cheap and, we thought, effective way of targeting our

core customer base. But last year, we had the good fortune to recruit a dynamic young Marketing Manager who brought with him a group of people who are changing the way we do things. We're looking to produce another even more successful series of TV commercials next year.

[pause]

Twenty

Spend money to earn money! That's been the philosophy of our organisation for years. The directors liked expensive-looking TV commercials, which appealed to our core customers in the old age bracket. However, our last campaign proved that you don't always have to go over budget to win new customers. We thought of a new approach, which our agency developed, and it turned out to be cheaper and, to our delight, brought us to the attention of a new, younger market.

[pause]

Twenty-one

Successful TV campaigns can be costly, and good market research is absolutely vital. We've always researched thoroughly before a campaign, but there's something else which was the key to last month's success. Although some people attribute it to our main rival's bankruptcy, it was the fact that we found a management group who we brought in to recommend ways of improving our marketing that really helped. A suggestion to use a TV campaign to advertise in-store promotions and mail-order facilities paid off handsomely.

[pause]

Twenty-two

Consultants recommended hiring a whole new marketing team for the company, but I rejected this. We've got a good experienced team in the company. It would've been an unnecessary expense. We decided we should put more effort into the groundwork for the campaign. Our team carried out a more detailed customer survey, and on the basis of that, our production company was able to create a commercial that was more accurately targeted.

[pause]

Now listen to the recordings again.

[pause]

That is the end of Part Two.

[pause]

Part Three. Questions 23 to 30.

You will hear a radio interview with a businessman called Brett Porter, who developed a product called Rainaway, a type of waterproof map.

For each question, 23–30, mark one letter (A, B or C) for the correct answer.

After you have listened once, replay the recording.

You have 45 seconds to read through the questions.

[pause]

Now listen, and mark A, B or C.

[pause]

Woman: . . . and today we're talking to Brett Porter, whose company developed the hugely successful all-weather maps called 'Rainaway'. These are waterproof maps that can be used by people who ride motorbikes. Brett, welcome to the programme.

Man: Thanks.

Woman: You actually invented Rainaway – how did that come about?

Man: Well, anyone, like me, who rides a motorbike, understands the problem of ordinary maps falling to pieces when it's raining or windy. There are three million bikers just in the UK, who I knew would be willing to pay for a solution to this problem. Nobody had ever produced something like Rainaway – I'd assumed it couldn't be done . . . that the costs were too great . . . but I was disappointed that my needs as a consumer weren't catered for, and people I knew kept encouraging me to develop and produce it as a business.

Woman: Was establishing the company difficult?

Man: In fact, I already had my own company – a motorcycle courier firm – but this was completely different and involved setting up a new business. What I'd learnt about pricing didn't seem to apply – I'd never dealt with a 'product' as such. But I knew I understood the market better than most. If I could make the product, I'd be meeting a demand. However, knowing *where* to sell and how to get it into the shops was another matter!

Woman: I see.

Man: But I was convinced the business would grow fast. I even entered the European Awards Scheme for ideas for business start-ups. It had a first prize of one hundred thousand euros' worth of software from Croner Consulting. The awards were sponsored by Alliance Business Bank – and because I made the final shortlist, I was offered a two-per-cent interest loan from them if I needed it. They organised a dinner for everyone on the shortlist, and I happened to get chatting to their senior business consultant, who gave me some invaluable financial advice. It really helped get me started.

Woman: Did you do any trial production of the maps?

Man: Yes. I knew what they should look like – a strong cover and small enough to flick through quickly. But trials took six months. The difficulty was we had to use a really tough kind of plastic for the cover, and this had to be fed into the printer sheet by sheet – fine for a small output, but absolutely no good for large-scale production.

Woman: Did you have any trouble persuading a printing company to make Rainaway?

Man: I thought I would – it wasn't really in a printer's interest to make a long-lasting product. The real difficulty, though, was my lack of a track record. They thought I was just planning a one-off print run or a very small-scale operation, which wouldn't be very profitable for them. Once I'd persuaded the boss of one firm that wasn't the case, he seemed willing to take a chance.

Woman: Do you use someone else's maps to make Rainaway from?

Man: Yes, we use Herne Publishing's. Of course, given they know they're a crucial supplier, there's a danger in a few years they might want to buy us out. But in the meantime, I have a protected trademark, and the people at Herne Publishing realise it's better for them to let me use my knowledge and contacts to establish the business. The alternative for them would involve spending money on producing a rival product, which I know they would be reluctant to do.

Woman: You must be pleased with Rainaway's performance?

Man: Absolutely. We launched Rainaway in September two thousand one, and sold two hundred thousand maps in the first year alone. In the last couple of years, the company turned over in excess of seven hundred thousand pounds, our best result so far, which isn't bad when you consider our maps retail at ten to twenty-four pounds each.

Woman: Very impressive! What's next for Rainaway? Do you plan to extend your range?

Man: I already have plenty of other ideas for the longer term, but that's all I can say for now. I've been devoting a lot of time recently to facilitating expansion by setting up a call centre to deal with mail-order sales. That's just opened, with a staff of twenty-five. I now need to concentrate on our advertisements – they've been very popular so far, but it's tough coming up with new ideas to continue to attract attention.

Woman: I wish you luck.

[pause]

Now listen to the recording again.

[pause]

That is the end of Part Three. You now have ten minutes to transfer your answers to your Answer Sheet.

Note: Teacher, stop the recording here and time ten minutes. Remind students when there is **one** minute remaining.

That is the end of the test.

Test 4   Reading

Part 1

1 B   2 A   3 B   4 D   5 C   6 A
7 C

Part 2

8 E   9 B   10 D   11 F   12 A

Part 3

13 B   14 A   15 B   16 B   17 C
18 A

Part 4

19 B   20 A   21 D   22 D   23 C
24 A   25 B   26 C   27 D   28 D
29 B   30 A   31 C   32 C   33 A

Part 5

34 THE   35 CORRECT   36 AND
37 FOR   38 UP   39 IT
40 CORRECT   41 OF   42 CORRECT
43 HAVE   44 WHO   45 BETWEEN

Test 4 Writing

Part 1

Sample A

> I have a piece of good news to inform you. I
> saw a new model of laser-printer on the
> exhibition of last week. It is beautiful and of
> good quality. Because many companies are
> very interested in it, I think we'd better make
> an order soon to replace the old one in our
> office.

Band 3

All content points are covered, and the range of
language is satisfactory. Both the format and
register are appropriate, and although there are
some errors, these do not obscure communication
of the message.

Sample B

> I am writing to suggest that we could buy an
> overhead projector I saw in an exhibition. It
> would be useful to do the presentations of the
> new products.
>
> The XP3 model has the latest technology and, if
> we order it soon, the supplier will grant us a
> 20% discount.
>
> Regards.

Band 5

All points are covered, and language is controlled
and concise, and demonstrates a wide lexical
range. The register is consistently appropriate, as is
the format.

Part 2

Sample C

> Report
>
> Our company is having problems with
> Sorenson, one of our main suppliers. The
> details of the problems are list below.
>
> Mainly there are 3 types of problem, late
> deliveries, unsatisfactory quality are errors with

> invoices. For the first one, late deliveries, the
> number of problems is 24. This figure is more
> than last year. For unsatisfactory quality, it is 17.
> Low quality products are more than before
> recently. The main factor is due the suppliers'
> unsatisfactory quality. The third one, errors with
> invoices, there are 7 problems. Therefore, in the
> future we must check all invoices from suppliers.
>
> I recommend that we should send a problem
> list to Sorenson and ask them to reduce the
> problems at the lowest level. If the similar
> problems happen in the future, we have to
> cancel the contract with Sorenson.

Band 2

The point concerning relative costs has not been
covered, and therefore the target reader would not
be fully informed. Otherwise, the language range
and cohesion are satisfactory, as are the format
and register. Although errors do occur, these do
not prevent the message being conveyed.

Sample D

> This report aims to recommend a solution to
> the problems with Sorenson, one of our
> suppliers.
>
> We find that three essential problems should be
> paid attention to: Firstly, twenty-four times of
> late deliveries, much more than last year, has
> caused a lot of inconvenience. Secondly, we are
> dissappointed about their unsatisfactory quality
> of goods which almost made us lose our
> customers. Thirdly errors with invoices brought
> us a lot of trouble.
>
> It is concluded that Sorenson's costs are nearly
> 30 per cent higher than those of our other
> suppliers.
>
> We recommend that we turn to other suppliers
> and make it a rule to check all invoices from
> suppliers in future. On the whole, we suggest a
> appropriate way to discuss it with Sorenson.

Band 4

All content points are covered, and the report is
well within the recommended word limit.
Language is generally accurate, and good range is
demonstrated. Both register and format are
appropriate and the report is well organised.

Test 4   Listening

Part 1

1 INTERNATIONAL COMMUNICATION
2 BOARDROOM
3 FEEDBACK FORM(S)
4 GLOBAL PARTNERSHIPS
5 HEADED
6 TRAINING SESSION
7 CHANGE SUPPLIER
8 INSTALMENTS
9 INNOVATIONS
10 HUMAN RESOURCES/HR
11 TEAMWORK
12 MOTIVATION

Part 2

13 D	14 B	15 E	16 A	17 F
18 G	19 H	20 A	21 E	22 C

Part 3

23 A	24 C	25 B	26 C	27 A
28 B	29 B	30 A		

Tapescript

Listening Test 4

This is the Business English Certificate Vantage 4, Listening Test 4.

Part One. Questions 1 to 12.

You will hear three telephone conversations or messages.

Write one or two words or a number in the numbered spaces on the notes or forms below.

After you have listened once, replay each recording.

[pause]

Conversation One. Questions 1 to 4.

Look at the note below.

You will hear a woman telephoning about a seminar

You have 15 seconds to read through the note.

[pause]

Now listen, and fill in the spaces.

[pause]

Man: Hello. Can I help you?

Woman: My name's Sue Bentley. Is Amy Johnson there?

Man: I'm afraid not. I'm her assistant. Can I take a message?

Woman: I'm running a seminar in Amy's department next Thursday. The provisional title was 'Dealing with Overseas Clients'. Could you please tell Amy I've changed it to 'International Communication' instead?

Man: Certainly. Anything else?

Woman: Yes. I've seen the rooms Amy recommended . . . I like the presentation room best, but it's too small for all twenty participants, so I'd better have the boardroom. One more thing: I can deal with photocopying the slides myself, but if Amy could provide photocopies of the feedback form for everyone, that'd be great.

Man: OK. Got that.

Woman: And could you also mention that she's welcome to keep hold of one of the books I've lent her – *Working Overseas* – but I do need the other one back in time for the seminar – it's called *Global Partnerships*. That's all! Thank you for your help.

Man: You're welcome.

[pause]

Now listen to the recording again.

[pause]

Conversation Two. Questions 5 to 8.

Look at the note below.

You will hear a man phoning about a delivery.

You have 15 seconds to read through the note.

[pause]

Now listen, and fill in the spaces.

[pause]

Man: Sarah Williams, please.

Woman: I'm afraid she's not available right now.

Man: Ah, can you ask her to call me back? Brian Jones – it's urgent.

Woman: Of course. Can I ask what it's about?

Man: You tell her there's been a mix-up yet again. Instead of plain paper, we've got headed paper. Last month, we even got lined paper!

Woman: I do apologise. I'll ask her to phone you as soon as possible. She's at lunch at the moment, and then she'll be in a training session, but I'll make sure she contacts you when that finishes.

Man: Ah, we need the goods by Thursday, otherwise our production line will be held up, and we'll miss our deadlines. If you can't sort it out, we'll have to change supplier. We can't afford to wait around.

Woman: Of course.

Man: And another thing – the amount owing on the invoice is given in full – that's not right.

I'd thought we'd agreed I'd settle the bill by instalments. I could pay half now, but I'm not prepared to.

Woman: I'm sure she can sort something out.

[pause]

Now listen to the recording again.

[pause]

Conversation Three. Questions 9 to 12.

Look at the notes below.

You will hear a journalist asking for information about a conference.

You have 15 seconds to read through the notes.

[pause]

Now listen, and fill in the spaces.

[pause]

Woman: New Vision, Conference Department, Janet Edwards speaking.

Man: Hello. This is Nick Brown from *Business News*. I hear you're running a rather special conference in Newcastle.

Woman: You mean our event on the tenth of October?

Man: Yes. Can you tell me something about it, so I can mention it in our paper?

Woman: Certainly. The name should give you a clue – we're calling it 'Innovations'. Not the usual 'Better Sales Techniques', etc.

Man: That sounds very forward-looking. I assume it's about new developments in technology?

Woman: We thought there were too many seminars on that. We're focusing on human resources instead.

Man: New ways of approaching it, I suppose. Interesting! So, who have you got to lead it?

Woman: Well, this is a little different, too – Daniel Christie.

Man: Is he the man from Cambridge Business School who's just written that book on incentive schemes?

Woman: I believe teamwork is actually his field.

Man: So, for example, the way people interact . . . Any other special features?

Woman: We're planning some practical and very unusual workshops about motivation. I think that'll cause a few surprises.

Man: How 'unusual'?

Woman: Come and see for yourself. I'll send you a complimentary ticket.

Man: Thank you. I will.

[pause]

Now listen to the recording again.

[pause]

That is the end of Part One. You now have 20 seconds to check your answers.

[pause]

Part Two. Questions 13 to 22.

Section One. Questions 13 to 17.

You will hear five short recordings.

For each recording, decide what way of improving profitability the speaker is recommending.

Write one letter (A–H) next to the number of the recording.

Do not use any letter more than once.

After you have listened once, replay the recordings.

You have 15 seconds to read the list A–H.

[pause]

Now listen, and decide what way of improving profitability each speaker is recommending.

[pause]

Thirteen

Sure, the relocation plan is attractive, but just look at the costs! And this just isn't a good time to be spending that sort of money. Why not make the most of what we've got, instead of starting from scratch? Keep our present location, strip it down, and completely redesign and redecorate our existing workspace. I think we could be far more efficient without such a huge outlay.

[pause]

Fourteen

Well, I feel that we're just not making enough profit to sustain the kind of growth we need. Obviously, production costs have increased, and I don't think we've taken that into account nearly enough. Introducing a competitive pricing strategy wouldn't mean that we couldn't take inflation into account, and we should certainly consider this before the end of the year. Otherwise, we'll find ourselves selling at below cost!

[pause]

Fifteen

Time equals money, and you just have to look at the amount of time we spend – well, waste – travelling from place to place to realise that this is costing us too much. We're duplicating a lot of services and systems, which we wouldn't have to do if we streamlined our offices. Operating from one location instead of four would lead to greater control, considerable reduction in costs and increased efficiency. Staff would appreciate it, too.

[pause]

Sixteen

I think that there's a danger – we're over-diversified and, instead of looking at our production processes and ways of automating them even further, what we should be doing is targeting our most successful lines and focusing on them, even if it means abandoning some lines altogether. What I'm talking about is specialisation – concentrate on what we know we do well and what we know will make money. And that'll bring down costs, too.

[pause]

Seventeen

We're relying too heavily on past success, without thinking about where we go from here. You can't just rely on maintaining productivity. Prices of raw materials are rising, and our overheads are enormous – look at what we're spending on buildings alone. In this business, you have to run just to stay in the same place. We've go to constantly improve, and that means getting more produced faster, and better.

[pause]

Now listen to the recordings again.

[pause]

Section Two. Questions 18 to 22.

You will hear another five recordings.

For each recording, decide what the speaker is trying to do.

Write one letter (A–H) next to the number of the recording.

Do not use any letter more than once.

After you have listened once, replay the recordings.

You have 15 seconds to read the list A–H.

[pause]

Now listen, and decide what each speaker is trying to do.

[pause]

Eighteen

I'm afraid we really need to finish the project as soon as possible. If we don't keep to the schedule, the delay could lose us our external funding. Losing that could lead to various problems, including salaries not being paid on time. Don't forget as well that the budget depends on us finishing by the end of the summer. No, we need to keep to our original plans and keep that money coming in.

[pause]

Nineteen

As you can see, the figures speak for themselves – our model EXG surpassed all forecasts in its first year. Because of our competitive pricing policy, it has been selling extremely well. However, we want to extend this trend and build on it. We now need to come up with a campaign to make sure we increase the number of models we sell abroad, not just on the domestic market. Japan is our main target.

[pause]

Twenty

Right, let's see where we've gotten to. We've agreed to recognise when staff have worked hard and achieved their goals. Sales need to have done reasonably well in their area – ideally better than the forecasts while keeping within budget. And, if we feel a person is worth substantial investment, we can go with a five-per-cent pay rise, as well as offering a bonus in exceptional circumstances.

[pause]

Twenty-one

The figures show quite clearly that we didn't reach the target we set last year. If anything, I think we ought to cut back on spending, at least for the next few months. If sales pick up in the new year and we manage to add new clients to our base, maybe we can think about buying more estate and equipment then. If I may say so, we have to be realistic.

[pause]

Twenty-two

What were last year's figures? Hm. Not too good, I see – sales in the US were down, but it looks as though they were more or less constant in Asia. However, the worldwide market's pretty buoyant at the moment, forecasts do seem more optimistic, and our investment looks sound, so yeah, let's go along with that – we'll allocate four hundred thousand dollars for the first quarter. That's an eight-per-cent increase on last year – we should be able to keep within that.

[pause]

Now listen to the recordings again.

[pause]

That is the end of Part Two.

[pause]

Part Three. Questions 23 to 30.

You will hear part of a tutorial between a business student called Gareth and his tutor, in which they discuss Trident Appliances, a manufacturer of photocopiers.

For each question, 23–30, mark one letter (A, B or C) for the correct answer.

After you have listened once, replay the recording.

You have 45 seconds to read through the questions.

[pause]

Now listen, and mark A, B or C.

[pause]

Woman: Ah, Gareth, do sit down.

Man: Thank you.

Woman: Now, presumably you've considered this case study about Trident Appliances?

Man: Yes.

Woman: Good. Well, let's start with the present situation. Trident manufactures photocopiers, which they sell in bulk to retailers and large organisations. Now, why do you think they're having trouble selling them?

Man: It's strange, because there's a big demand for photocopiers, and Trident's are competitively priced. But the specifications just don't compare with what's expected these days. It's a shame, because they've got plenty of technical expertise in their engineering support team.

Woman: OK. Now, the company is owned by a large multinational. How do they see Trident?

Man: Well, the group is largely in the mining sector, and Trident doesn't fit in with that, so you'd expect the parent company to want to sell it. Or alternatively to be active, say by helping it to expand its markets. But really it seems quite content to take a hands-off approach, as long as Trident is generating some income.

Woman: Hmm . . . There's clearly poor morale among the employees. Why do you think that is?

Man: Well, weak line managers are often a reason, but I can't find any evidence for that here. And even the recent changes, like the cut in bonuses, have been accepted fairly calmly. I think it reflects people's uncertainty about their long-term prospects with the company.

Woman: What would you say about the sales staff? There's a lot about them in the case study.

Man: They're doing the best they can in the circumstances. There's a system for helping them to develop their selling skills, and that's working. The way customers are allocated to each salesperson could be improved maybe, to reduce unnecessary travel. But they're getting contradictory signals about what they're supposed to be doing: just responding to enquiries, or going out looking for new business.

Woman: Uh-huh. And what about the service engineers: what's the main weakness in that department?

Man: They seem to miss a lot of opportunities. When they visit a customer to install or repair a photocopier, it's their chance to look at all the equipment there and suggest how Trident could supply the company's needs better. Then there's their problem with spares, the Parts Services Department keeps stocks low, for financial reasons, but that means the engineers often can't get the parts they need for call-outs, and the customer has to wait.

Woman: Now, what about communications within the company? I'm sure you'll agree they're not as good as they could be. Why do you think that is?

Man: Well, was bit surprised, because, in fact, middle managers hold regular meetings with their departments. But that's because they're given information by the top management about policy issues and plans, for instance, which they have to pass on. But I have to say that some of them don't seem to think their staff can have anything to say that's worth hearing. And, of course, this creates ill feeling.

Woman: OK. Now, if you think about the Chief Executive's problems for a moment . . . what do you think he needs to tackle first?

Man: There are so many problems! Something needs to be done about the workforce, because some departments employ staff without the necessary training. In the long term, of course, they need to develop the photocopiers themselves. But the priority must be to reverse the fall in revenue, even if it means cutting prices, in order to increase the sales volume. Unless they do that, they'll go out of business very soon.

Woman: And what about their advertising?

Man: Well, they're using modern media, like the internet, and targeting their advertising more than they used to, for instance by moving from magazine ads to direct mailshots to companies. But these have an old-fashioned feel to them; the layout and graphics don't seem to have changed for twenty years.

Woman: Right. Now, let's go on to . . .

[pause]

Now listen to the recording again.

[pause]

That is the end of Part Three. You now have ten minutes to transfer your answers to your Answer Sheet.

[pause]

Note: Teacher, stop the recording here and time ten minutes. Remind students when there is **one** minute remaining.

That is the end of the test.

INTERLOCUTOR FRAMES

To facilitate practice for the Speaking test, the scripts followed by the interlocutor for Parts 2 and 3 appear below. They should be used in conjunction with Tests 1–4 Speaking tasks. These tasks are contained in booklets in the real Speaking test.

Interlocutor frames are not included for Part 1, in which the interlocutor asks the candidates questions directly rather than asking them to perform tasks.

Part 2: Mini presentations (about six minutes)

Interlocutor:
• Now, in this part of the test I'm going to give each of you a choice of three different topics. I'd like you to select one of the topics and give a short presentation on it for about a minute. You will have a minute to prepare this and you can make notes if you wish. After you have finished your talk, your partner will ask you a question.
• All right? Here are your topics. Please don't write anything in the booklet.

[Interlocutor hands each candidate a booklet and a pencil and paper for notes.]

Interlocutor:
• Now, B, which topic have you chosen, A, B or C?
• Would you like to talk about what you think is important when *[interlocutor states candidate's chosen topic]*? A, please listen carefully to B's talk and then ask him/her a question about it.

[Candidate B speaks for one minute.]

Interlocutor:
• Thank you. Now, A, please ask B a question about his/her talk.

[Candidate A asks a question.]

Interlocutor:
• Now, A, which topic have you chosen, A, B or C?
• Would you like to talk about what you think is important when *[interlocutor states candidate's chosen topic]*? B, please listen carefully to A's talk and then ask him/her a question about it.

[Candidate A speaks for one minute.]

Interlocutor:
• Thank you. Now, B, please ask A a question about his/her talk.

[Candidate B asks a question.]

Interlocutor:
• Thank you.
• Can I have the booklets, please?

Part 3: Collaborative task and discussion (about seven minutes)

Interlocutor:
• Now, in this part of the test, you are going to discuss something together.

[Interlocutor holds the Part 3 booklet open at the task while giving the instructions below.]

Interlocutor:
• You have 30 seconds to read this task carefully, and then about three minutes to discuss and decide about it together. You should give reasons for your decisions and opinions. You don't need to write anything. Is that clear?

[Interlocutor places the booklet in front of the candidates so they can both see it.]

Interlocutor:
• I'm just going to listen and then ask you to stop after about three minutes. Please speak so that we can hear you.

[Candidates have about three minutes to complete the task.]

Interlocutor:
• Can I have the booklet, please?

[Interlocutor asks one or more of the following questions as appropriate, to extend the discussion.]

Examples:
• Do you think magazines are a good way to keep staff informed? (Why?/Why not?)
• Do you think companies of all sizes should have staff magazines? (Why?/Why not?)
• Is it important for senior managers to contribute to staff magazines? (Why?/Why not?)
• Would you like to contribute to staff magazines? (Why?/Why not?)
• Do you think an internal company website would be a good way of keeping staff informed? (Why?/Why not?)
• Do you think magazines for customers are a useful marketing tool? (Why?/Why not?)

• Thank you. That is the end of the test.

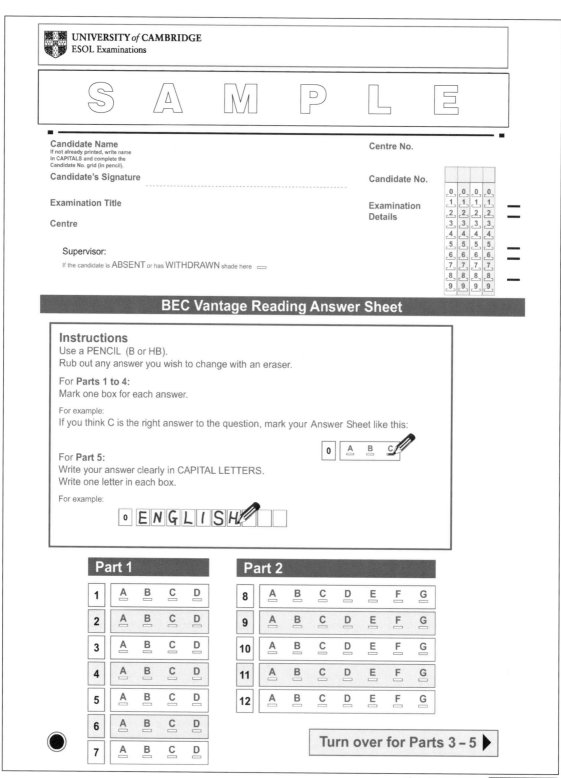

Part 3

	A	B	C	D
13	☐	☐	☐	☐
14	☐	☐	☐	☐
15	☐	☐	☐	☐
16	☐	☐	☐	☐
17	☐	☐	☐	☐
18	☐	☐	☐	☐

Part 4

	A	B	C	D
19	☐	☐	☐	☐
20	☐	☐	☐	☐
21	☐	☐	☐	☐
22	☐	☐	☐	☐
23	☐	☐	☐	☐
24	☐	☐	☐	☐
25	☐	☐	☐	☐
26	☐	☐	☐	☐

	A	B	C	D
27	☐	☐	☐	☐
28	☐	☐	☐	☐
29	☐	☐	☐	☐
30	☐	☐	☐	☐
31	☐	☐	☐	☐
32	☐	☐	☐	☐
33	☐	☐	☐	☐

Part 5

34		1 34 0	
35		1 35 0	
36		1 36 0	
37		1 37 0	
38		1 38 0	
39		1 39 0	
40		1 40 0	
41		1 41 0	
42		1 42 0	
43		1 43 0	
44		1 44 0	
45		1 45 0	

© UCLES 2009 Photocopiable

UNIVERSITY *of* **CAMBRIDGE**
ESOL Examinations

S A M P L E

Candidate Name
If not already printed, write name
in CAPITALS and complete the
Candidate No. grid (in pencil).

Candidate's Signature

Examination Title

Centre

Supervisor:
If the candidate is ABSENT or has WITHDRAWN shade here ▭

Centre No.

Candidate No.

Examination Details

0	0	0	0
1	1	1	1
2	2	2	2
3	3	3	3
4	4	4	4
5	5	5	5
6	6	6	6
7	7	7	7
8	8	8	8
9	9	9	9

BEC Vantage Listening Answer Sheet

Instructions
Use a PENCIL (B or HB).
Rub out any answer you wish to change with an eraser.

For **Part 1:**
Write your answer clearly in CAPITAL LETTERS.
Write one letter or number in each box.
If the answer has more than one word, leave one box empty between words.

For example:

`0` `Q U E S T I O N   1 2`

For **Parts 2 and 3:**
Mark one box for each answer.

For example:
If you think C is the right answer to the question, mark your Answer Sheet like this:

`0` | A | B | C̲ |

Part 1 - Conversation One

1 [ ]
1 1 0

2 [ ]
1 2 0

3 [ ]
1 3 0

4 [ ]
1 4 0

Continue on the other side of this sheet ▶

© UCLES 2009 Photocopiable

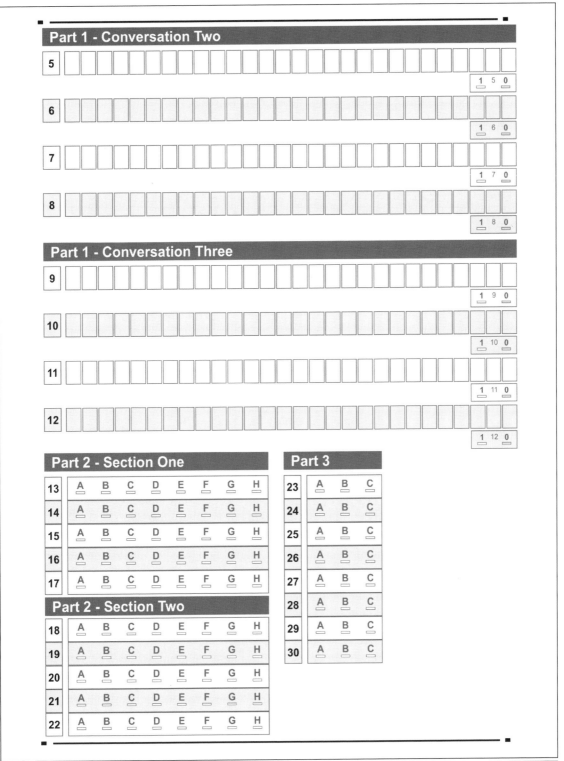

Part 1 - Conversation Two

5   1   5   0

6   1   6   0

7   1   7   0

8   1   8   0

Part 1 - Conversation Three

9   1   9   0

10   1   10   0

11   1   11   0

12   1   12   0

Part 2 - Section One

13	A	B	C	D	E	F	G	H
14	A	B	C	D	E	F	G	H
15	A	B	C	D	E	F	G	H
16	A	B	C	D	E	F	G	H
17	A	B	C	D	E	F	G	H

Part 2 - Section Two

18	A	B	C	D	E	F	G	H
19	A	B	C	D	E	F	G	H
20	A	B	C	D	E	F	G	H
21	A	B	C	D	E	F	G	H
22	A	B	C	D	E	F	G	H

Part 3

23	A	B	C
24	A	B	C
25	A	B	C
26	A	B	C
27	A	B	C
28	A	B	C
29	A	B	C
30	A	B	C

© UCLES 2009   Photocopiable

Thanks and acknowledgements

The authors and publishers acknowledge the following sources of copyright material and are grateful for the permissions granted. While every effort has been made, it has not always been possible to identify the sources of all the material used, or to trace all copyright holders. If any omissions are brought to our notice, we will be happy to include the appropriate acknowledgements on reprinting.

Steven Sonsino for the adapted text on p. 19 'The stars of the future'. Originally published in *People Management* 3 April 2003. Reproduced by kind permission of Steven Sonsino (www.stevensonsino.com); NI Syndication for the adapted text on p. 22 'Creativity in the workplace' from 'Staff turn on the creativity tap' *The Times* 11 January 2001, for the adapted text on p. 80 'When two brands are better than one' *The Times* 24 April 2002. Copyright © NI Syndication 2002, 2003; Tim Hitchcock for the adapted text on p. 40 'The best person for the job' *The Guardian* 6 January 2003. Reproduced by permission of Tim Hitchcock; Management Today for the adapted text on p. 42 'Critical path' from 'How to drag your company back from the brink' written by Andrew Saunders, *Management Today* September 2002. Reproduced by permission of Andrew Saunders, Management Today; The Guardian for the adapted text on p. 60 'Issues in the recruitment world' from 'Head start: Local government is increasingly calling on specialist recruitment companies to find the top-quality executives who are so much in demand' by Simon Parker, *The Guardian* 2 April 2003. Copyright © Guardian News & Media Limited, 2003; adapted text on p. 82 'Speaking your customers' language', written by Catherine Cook, *Business Age*.